# STOCK MARKET INVESTING

Start Investing Today and Secure Your Financial Future

(A Complete and Ultimate Crash Course on Stock Markets)

**Anshul Karwa**

Published by Knowledge Icons

© **Anshul Karwa**

All Rights Reserved

*Stock Market Investing: Start Investing Today and Secure Your Financial Future (A Complete and Ultimate Crash Course on Stock Markets)*

ISBN 978-1-990084-83-6

**Legal & Disclaimer**

The information contained in this book is not designed to replace or take the place of any form of medicine or professional medical advice. The information in this book has been provided for educational and entertainment purposes only.

The information contained in this book has been compiled from sources deemed reliable, and it is accurate to the best of the Author's knowledge; however, the Author cannot guarantee its accuracy and validity and cannot be held liable for any errors or omissions. Changes are periodically made to this book. You must consult your doctor or get professional medical advice before using any of the suggested remedies, techniques, or information in this book.

# Table of Contents

# Table of Contents

# Introduction

There are many benefits to investing in the stock market. It is for this reason that people religiously follow the market and invest in stocks. Before they do that, they try to find all the material that they can about investing in the stock market to try their hand. Little do they know that they should only use those sources that are trustworthy and reliable. If you have always wanted to give investing in the stock market a shot, you have come to the right place. Some people will not have the required funds to invest in the market. But, did you know that you do not need more than $10 to invest in the stock market? You must ensure that you choose the right shares to invest in. Most people want to invest in the stock market so they can save funds for their retirement. What you need to understand is that the securities in the stock market are volatile. The price of these instruments will change because of some news or changes in the regulations. This goes to show that any little change can also lead to price volatility. So, what do you do in such situations? Do you still invest in the market, or do you pull out quickly? This book will tell you precisely what you need to do and how you need to do it. Throughout this book, you will gather information on what the stock market is and why it is a good idea to invest in the market. We will also look at different trading strategies and techniques you can use to invest in the stock market. You will also learn how you can make it big since you can make a huge profit when you invest in stocks. The book will leave you with some tips and tricks that you can use to invest successfully in the market and make profits. You must pay attention to how to invest in stocks, so you do not make any mistakes when you invest. This book also sheds some light on trading in stocks and everything else you need to know about stock investing. It is okay to make occasional mistakes when you invest in stocks. You cannot, however, make the same mistakes every time. If you do this, you will find it difficult to make profits. You must ensure that you always learn from your experiences since that is the only way to make profits. We will also look at some common mistakes that people tend to make when they invest in stocks. You must do your best to avoid making the same mistakes repeatedly.

# Chapter 1: All You Need To Know About Stock Market As A Beginner.

Make it a point to set realistic trading objectives

Before you decide to make your very first investment, try to ask yourself the following questions. At what point will you require the money you have invested? Will it be after 6 months, a year, 5 years or perhaps much longer?, Are you trying to lay a nest egg for your sunset years?, Are seeking to obtain the necessary funds to finance your college education or perhaps seeking money to buy a home? On the other hand, do wish to establish an estate that you want to leave for your beneficiaries upon your demise?

Whichever the case, prior to making any investment, you ought to fully determine your primary driving motivation. When you have ascertained this critical point, next consider the most likely time in the future you might stand in need of the funds you wish to invest. Should you require your investment back within just a couple of years, then it will be much better to consider another investment channel. It is very important for you to fully understand that the stock market with its volatility can offer no guarantee on just when your investment will be made available.

Accordingly, you should always make it a point to calculate beforehand how much cash you wish to invest and what kind of ROI you may deem suitable to realize your trading objectives. As a rule of thumb, always recall that the eventual growth of your stock market portfolio relies on 3 interdependent factors. These are the exact capital you decide to invest, the amount of yearly earnings on your investment. And lastly, the exact number of years you wish to invest your capital in the stock markets.

Take the necessary time to effectively determine your risk tolerance

Risk tolerance happens to be a psychological attribute, which is genetically oriented. Yet, it can still be significantly influenced by factors such as education, income or even wealth. The moment all these factors increase in value; risk tolerance also tends to rise. Basically, your exact level of risk tolerance can be accurately described as how you feel about any risk you make. As well as the exact level of anxiety you tend to experience whenever you decide to undertake risky ventures. Take your time to ask yourself, Can I risk $100 to gain $1,000 or perhaps $1000 to gain $1,000?

It is vital for you to fully understand that all people possess varying levels of risk tolerance. This certainly means that there is no such thing as 'right balance' in this given issue.

At the same time, risk tolerance can generally be influenced with the exact 'perception' of the risk an individual is contemplating to take. This given concept of risk tolerance is then the most accurate when it comes to stock market investment or trading. As you become well conversant with the basics of trading, you will find that the idea of the risks involved in such matters is generally lesser. This includes having an excellent understanding of how to buy and sell stocks, assessing market volatility (price changes). Along with the ease or difficulties of liquidating stock market investments.

This usually leads to a lessening of the overall anxiety you are bound to experience when you trade or invest in the stock market, due to your 'perception' of the risks involved. So, by taking the necessary time to fully understand your exact risk tolerance, you will be able to avoid trading in investments you dread. Ideally, you should not invest in an asset which has the potential to cause you sleepless nights. Anxiety triggers fear that in its turn prompts an emotional response to the stressor. By always retaining a cool head during stock market uncertainty, you will be able to adhere to an 'unemotional' decision-making process in your stock market activities.

Make it a habit to keep off your emotions from your investments

By far the largest obstacle quite a large number of beginners have to routinely face is their inability to regulate their emotions and proceed to make logical decisions. In the short term, the prices of company stocks correspond with the combined emotions of the whole investment community. When most stock market investors happen to be anxious about a particular firm, its stock prices will be bound to take a plunge. Alternatively, when most traders possess a positive perspective to a firm, its stock prices will naturally rise.

Those individuals who retain a negative perspective about the stock market are known as 'bears'. While those that have positive outlooks to the same are known as 'bulls.' During market hours, the unceasing struggle between bulls and bears is usually reflected on the constantly fluctuating securities' prices. These short term fluctuations generally arise from rumors, speculations and in some cases even hope. All of these factors can be rightly labeled as been emotions. Effective stock market investment necessitates a logical and systematic analysis of a company's assets, management and future prospects.

At this juncture, it is important for you to remember that stock market prices can move in contrast to most expectations. For the inexperienced, this can fuel insecurity and tension. At such moments, you will find yourself faced with a dilemma - Should you sell your position to prevent a loss?, Or should you continue maintaining your position in the hope that the prices will ultimately rebound? Even in the occasions that prices perform as you expected, you will still find yourself facing troubling questions. Should you take a profit now prior to the prices falling?, Or should you maintain your position as the prices could rise even higher?

Dealing with all these perplexing thoughts can trigger a lot of worry, particularly if you constantly monitor the prices of the securities you trade in. This emotion can eventually prompt you take certain actions. As your emotions are the main motivation, it is mostly likely your action will be wrong. When you buy a stock, you should only do so for valid reasons. Also, you should have realistic expectations of exactly how the prices will perform if your guiding reasons prove to be accurate. Finally, before investing in any stock, always take time to determine the exact point you will liquidate your holdings, especially if your reasons are proven wrong. All in all, always have an appropriate 'exit' strategy prior to purchasing any stock, and make it a point to execute it unemotionally.

Make it your business to comprehensively learn about the basics of stock market investment

Prior to making your very first stock market investment or trade, make sure that you fully understand all the basics of stock market together with the individual securities which make them up. Below are some of the most pertinent areas you will be obliged to be well conversant with before commencing any stock market activities.

To begin with, take time to understand the exact financial metrics as well as definition that are utilized in stock market trading. Some of the most notable of which are P/E ratio, earnings / share, return on equity and compound annual growth rate. Take you time to fully grasp how these metrics are usually calculated. It is important to state that been in a position of effectively contrasting just how companies use these metrics is essential in any successful stock market investment operations.

Next you should learn all about the most popular techniques of stock selection and timing. To this end, you should make it a point to understand how fundamental and technical analysis can be executed. More importantly, just how they vary and when it is appropriate to use them in a stock market trading strategy. You should also be well conversant with the different types of stock market orders. Take all the time you require to fully comprehend just how market orders, limit orders, stop market orders, stop limit orders and trailing stop loss orders vary from each other.

Finally, you should make it a point to learn all you can on the different kinds of stock market investment accounts which are made available. You perhaps are well conversant with cash accounts that are arguably the most prevalently used by stock market investors. Nevertheless, what are known as margin accounts are by regulations, required when you wish to make some specific types of stock market trades. So, make sure you fully understand how margin accounts can be calculated. You should also find out about the exact differences between initial and maintenance margin accounts prerequisites.

## Make it a point to diversify your stock market investments

The moment you have performed all the necessary research that helps you determine and even quantify risk, making the decision to diversify your stock market portfolio can be a very shrewd step. The same is also the case, when you are totally 'comfortable' that you will be able to pinpoint any potential danger which might jeopardize your position in a stress-free manner. In both scenarios, you will be able to liquidate your stock market investments prior to sustaining any dangerous loss.

Therefore, the most prudent means of been able to effectually manage stock market investment risks is to diversify your exposure. You should know that most shrewd stock market investors, make it their business to own stocks from different firms, different sectors and even different nations. The primary driving force which motivates them to do so is the firm guarantee that a single inauspicious event can never influence all their holdings. What all this really boils down to is the undeniable fact that stock diversification can allow to comfortably recover from the loss of a single and even several of your investments.

Investing In Stock Market

Investing in the stock market and making money consistently and in large quantities is something that most dream of. The legendary Warren Buffet was in India a few months back and tomes and more tomes have been written on the methods that he adopts to make money in the stock market. His idea of value investing, which he credits to his mentor Benjamin Graham, has many followers. In this book we look at some of the important aspects that you need to be aware of while investing in the stock market. The book is for beginners and for an investment horizon of 3-5 years. The article is specific for Indian investors though most of the ideas expressed are universal.

Investing in Stock markets

Investing in the stock market gives superior returns over the long term and is more tax efficient than all other forms of investment. If done rightly you can get a return of 12-15% over the long term. You can either invest directly or through mutual funds. Stock market investing requires patience, risk-taking capability and time. Never invest on tips or just because a particular company is the flavor of the season. Reading financial reports and checking financial ratios may not be easy for everybody but you could look at a few things before making that investment.

Going by your gut instinct is good if you have long experience in picking stocks and if you keep in touch with news flow on what is going on in the sector or the particular company. If you are a beginner it is better to test your hypothesis with some data before you jump in to buy. It would be a good idea to start reading a business magazine which gives in-depth articles about companies or a particular sector.

If your investment decision is based on recommendations by some popular business news channels, then the outcome may not be very positive. It is best to take information from all media, do some study yourself, arrive at your own conclusion and start investing. Stock Market investing is not rocket science and if you can keep in mind a few points, you too, can pick up good stocks and reap the benefits of higher returns. If you plan to invest in the stock market, then the first lesson is to cultivate patience and humility. Try not to invest when the market is running up. Do not think that you will lose the opportunity and buy at a higher price. Always time your purchase when sharp corrections take place. Always remember that success does not beget success in the stock market. Do not be overconfident if you get a few picks right.

Choosing a company to invest

There are more than 6,000 stocks listed in the Bombay Stock Exchange and over 1,200 stocks listed in the National Stock Exchange. Many are listed on both. The stock exchange itself takes the best stocks [30 for BSE Sensex and 50 for Nifty] to make the index and usually picks the companies that are consistently profitable and those that have good corporate governance and show consistent performance. So one easy way out is to select a few among these index stocks in a downturn.

Another method would be to check the last quarter performance and then select a few companies that have shown good growth in sales and profitability. You can get this data from moneycontrol.com (website) or stock specific magazines like Capital Market or Dalal Street. Then look at quarterly performance over, say last 4-6 quarters and see if operations are improving. Look for consistent sales, operating profit and net profit numbers. A rising interest cost without a significant rise in sales in the subsequent quarters will indicate that the capital is not being deployed efficiently. If other income is contributing to a big chunk of the profit, be cautious. Do not go for companies which have mountains of debt. You can check this in the balance sheet or just by looking at the interest being paid from the quarterly result statements. In this way you could get a fix on a list of stocks that you need to keep watch on. Once you have a list of companies ready, visit their websites and check out the products they make. Search the Internet for news on the selected companies. Make a start, put in maybe 1 hour a week and you will soon be surprised to find that stock picking is not as difficult as you thought.

While buying the selected company fix an amount you would like to commit to a particular stock and allot about 50% of the money and then watch the movement. Please do not get into the habit of monitoring daily. You can do it on weekends and incase the stock moves down you could steadily increase your holding. If it runs away do not jump and invest the balance; wait for it to stabilize and see if it offers value at the higher price. Time your buys in a falling market and sells in a rising market

Profit Booking

Warren Buffet's philosophy is to buy a stock and sleep on it and reap value. It is often mistaken that Warren Buffet never sells his stocks. This is not true. He is an exceptional stock picker, so unlike us he starts with a big advantage. But he too reviews his investments and sells ones that make money or deviates from his stringent criteria. I would recommend that once you have picked up a stock and it has risen more than 25-50% [you can decide on the limit] you should sell maybe 10-15% of your position. This helps you to recover the capital until you fine tune your stock selection and learn your ropes in the fine art of stock selection. You could temporarily move this profit to a fixed income instrument for further investment in the same stock or any other during the next correction or switch to some other company that you have identified. Never have any emotional attachment to a stock.

Day trading /Short term trading

Stock market investing comes at the higher end of the risk spectrum. If you think that making money every day by buying and selling on the same day [day trading] and for the short term [within 1 year] is easy, it is fraught with greater risk. In the short term, stock market movements are volatile and impossible to predict. You may think you are an expert at spreadsheets and reading graphs but most of the time it is like throwing a dice. A few can do it but they usually make money more out of years of experience in analyzing daily movements. If you plan to do day trading be extremely cautious. Never do day trading on tips. If you are doing short term or day trading, you should never keep your loss making companies with the hope that one day it will give you profits. Sell and move on if the loss is more than 5 %. Likewise, if your position is profitable start selling in two or three lots if the market has a rising trend.

Stock market investing if done with discipline, can give extremely good returns. With diligence and patience, you can easily get the hang of picking up stocks. Just like in sports or for that matter any discipline, you need constant practice and an effort to update your knowledge. If that is done you are well on your way to successful stock picking.

Where Do You Start?

I've been at the investment game for a while now and I've reached the stage where I prefer to invest in the stock market via individual stocks rather than collective investment vehicles like unit or investment trusts. The main reason for this is that I'd prefer not to pay other people to do something that I know I can do better myself.

Of course, it wasn't always this way. It's taken me a quarter of a century of experience playing the markets to evolve my own profitable investment strategy. When I first started out though, like most people, I didn't have the confidence to take my own decisions. More important than that, I didn't have a large lump sum to play with in order to diversify my holdings sufficiently and build in a measure of safety. I suspect that's the position that most newcomers to the world of investing find themselves in.

So I'm not ashamed to admit that my first foray into the markets all those years ago was through one of the regular savings schemes run by the big investment trusts. Twenty-five years on I'd have to say that if I were just starting out on my investment journey now, I'd do exactly the same thing.

Why Investment Trusts?

Note that I chose investment trusts, not unit trusts. Although these two investment vehicles both allow investors to access a diversified portfolio of stocks with relatively small amounts of money, in my view, investment trusts have three clear advantages over their unit trust rivals:

1. Their management charges are lower.

2. Their long term performance is generally far better.

3. They can often be bought at a discount to their net asset value.

So if you're now scratching your head and wondering why, despite all these advantages, you've never heard of investment trusts, you're in very good company. Although things are slowly changing, investment trusts remain a closed book to most investors because, unlike their unit trust cousins, they don't pay commission to financial advisors. As a result, they're virtually ignored by the financial press. Let's face it, high commissions equal high advertising budgets and since the Sunday papers rely on advertising to boost sales, they'll happily provide favorable coverage in their money supplements to products promoted by high-spending advertisers. That sounds like a nice copy relationship between the big investment houses and the financial media, but it leaves the small investor out in the cold as usual - deprived of information about one of today's best-kept investment secrets. Hopefully, I'm about to help change all that.

If I've convinced you that investment trusts are worth investigating further, and you're ready to put your foot on that first rung of the investment ladder, then I've dug out a few options below which I believe would make ideal solutions for first-time investors like you. I've selected a range of vintage trusts with impeccable pedigrees from the broad global growth sector. These trusts offer a very low-cost way to access a broad, globally diversified portfolio. Rest assured that they all offer a regular monthly savings option for investors of more modest means:

Foreign & Colonial Investment Trust

1. First up is a trust that was my first choice when I started investing a quarter of a century ago and it's still going strong. It's the Foreign and Colonial Investment Trust, it allows minimum monthly savings of £50 per month and it's currently trading at a discount of 9.6% to net assets - which means that for every £90.40 invested, you're getting £100 worth of shares. Now these discounts can fluctuate a bit. It may be that next month the discount widens to 11% or 12% - which simply means that if you're a regular monthly investor, you get even more discounted shares for your money. Alternatively, the discount could narrow or even slip over into a premium as sometimes happens if a trust is particularly popular with investors - thus giving your investments a boost if you bought at a discount. Over the long term, however, whether you're a lump sum investor or a regular saver, it would be hard to go wrong with this trust as, over the last 3 years, your investment would have increased by 52.7% - not bad,

although past returns are no guarantee of a similar performance in future.

Witan

2. An alternative to the Foreign and Colonial Trust, but one which does virtually the same job, is a trust called Witan. It's performed even better than the Foreign and Colonial Trust with a return of 64.2% to investors over the last 3 years. It's also slightly cheaper, trading at a 10.14% discount to NAV (Net Asset Value). On paper then, a slightly better bet. Again, you can start saving from just £50 per month.

SAINTS

3. Finally, you could take a look at another old and well established stalwart, this time from the global growth and income category, and that's SAINTS, or the Scottish American Investment Trust. This too allows minimum monthly investments of £50 per month through its parent company, Baillie Gifford, and has performed outstandingly over the last 3

years, returning 107.6% to its lucky investors. The downside is that this performance didn't go unnoticed and the trust now stands at a premium to net assets of 4.1%. If you're looking for income though, this trust currently yields over 4%, so not a bad alternative to a building society provided you're prepared to risk your capital.

Whichever option you choose, provided you're in the markets for the long term, as you should be if you want to make decent returns, I think it would be very difficult to lose money with any of these trusts. That's doubly true if you're making regular monthly investments as you get the advantage of pound cost averaging, which means you buy more shares when prices dip, thus increasing your returns when shares subsequently rise. A few years down the line, once you feel you've accumulated enough in these well-diversified, low cost trusts, you can start dabbling in individual shares like I did.

So if you were thinking of dipping a toe in today's rather choppy investment waters, but either don't yet have a large enough lump sum, or are too scared to dive in and commit it right now, then I don't think you can do worse than follow my example: play it safe and set up an investment trust monthly savings scheme.

# Chapter 2: How The Stock Market Works

When you learned to drive, you didn't just jump in the car and turn it on. Instead, someone walked you through exactly what to do before you started the car. You were told what the stick-shift or automatic PRNDL was for. You were told how to move the mirrors, what was forward and reverse, and other buttons in the car. Before you invest in the stock market, you need to walk, not run. You need a guide that tells you how things work, so you avoid making costly mistakes. As long as you know how something works, you don't have to be afraid of the reality of it. Many people do not understand investing, so the stock market scares them. The reality is—you just need to know how it works, the parts that make it work, and you can set up an investment strategy that works.

A stock is usually referred to as a share. It is a share in a company that is looking for investors. These investors provide capital for the company to grow the company. When a company first offers shares it is called an IPO or Initial Public Offering. The share price is set on the estimated worth of the company, as well as the number of shares available for sale.

For the shares to be publicly offered, a company needs to be listed on a stock exchange, like the NYSE. Traders and investors can then buy and sell stocks, but the company will only make money with the IPO. After the IPO is over, it is simply businessmen, individuals, and investors trading the stocks between themselves to make a profit and dividends.

Buying Shares on the Stock Market

Investors and traders sell stocks after the IPO based on the perceived value. A company's value can go up or down, which is where investors make their money. A company's stock price that rises can provide a profit. If an investor has purchased those shares and the price or company value decreases, then the investor will lose money. It is also the investors and traders that will push the price in an up or down direction.

Investors have one of two goals: investing in the short or the long term. A long term investment is based on a stock continuing to rise in price. A short term investment is to gain quick cash, and pulling out before the stock price decreases.

Mature companies offer dividends to their shareholders. If you have stocks, then you are a shareholder in a company. If you hold the stocks long enough and have enough stock in a company, you can vote on new board members. Dividends are company profits that you get a cut of.

Investors will make money on the price fluctuations and the dividends. A seller is often trying to gain a profit by selling to a new buyer. The new buyer is also trying to buy in as low as possible, so that when the stock price continues to increase, they will make a profit.

The profit is calculated by taking the initial buy-in price and subtracting it from the closing or sale price. For example, if you buy into Google at $400 and wait for it to go up to $600, then the profit is $200 per share.

Sellers can push the price down due to supply and demand. This financial market works based on supply and demand.

Supply and Demand Concept

You should already know that in economics, when there is an oversupply of a product, the price is low. There is no demand for the product; therefore, a company or in this case a stock is not of interest.

When there is an undersupply of something like a stock, the demand is high. With more interested parties, a price will continue to increase.

If there is an even amount of supply and demand, then equality exists and there is no movement to see.

For the stock market, when too many people sell a stock, the price will decline. When too many people buy a stock the price will continue to rise. If there is an equal number of shares and interest, then the price usually trades sideways because there is a balance.

As you learn about the stock market, you will hear the word volume, often. Volume is the number of shares that change hands on a daily basis. Millions of shares can be traded on the stock exchange in a day as investors attempt to make money from increasing or decreasing prices.

The stock market works based on the interest or volume of traders. If a stock does not have any volume or very little, then it is not being actively traded, thus the price is not moving. Traders such as market makers get into the market in order to buy or sell stocks for companies with low volume. They do not stop a stock from rising or falling. Instead, market makers just try to garner interest in the company's stock.

What Most People Do

When it comes to the stock market and traders, most individuals are looking for the high volume trades, with fluctuating prices. They get in, make a profit, and get out to find the next big profit.

Final Thoughts

The shares are first released from a company to gain investment funds. The shares are then traded as a way to garner dividends and profit from the up and down trends in the market. The market also allows for you to invest on various exchanges around the world, as long as your broker provides access. Most people trade in their country's stock market or the largest in their region like the Japan Stock Exchange, London Stock Exchange and NYSE.

# Chapter 3: Picking Out Stocks To Invest In

After taking some time to research the stock market and what it has to offer, it is important that you take the time to pick out the right stocks. There are thousands of companies available on the stock market, but not all of them will provide you with a good return on investment. Some will provide you with one of the best opportunities to make money without all the risk and others will be failures right from the beginning. As a beginner, you may be worried about how you will sort these out so that you can pick the right stocks to make the most money for you.

The first thing that you should look at when you are ready to join the stock market is that you should never just pick out a stock, no matter what the circumstances are, simply because you heard through the grapevine or from a friend of a friend that the stock was a good one. Doing your own research is important. You can take the advice of other people, such as friends who are in the stock market and your broker, but remember that this is your investment and you need to be the one in control of it. Do some of your own research on the market, and you will soon learn which stocks are the best ones for your needs, regardless of what other people say.

If you have already done some research and have come up with a list of companies that you want to look at some more and possibly invest in, make sure to take some time searching on their website. Most of them will have information about their stocks, and this can be helpful when making your decision. You need to take a look at all of their reports on finances if possible to because this tells you how the company has done so far on the market. You will be surprised at how much information you are able to get about a company just by snooping around a little bit.

While there are a lot of things that you will need to consider when it comes to picking out a stock to work with, you need to go with one that will actually make you money in the process. Never pick a stock that is obviously going to cost you more than you can earn and try to go with the ones that are winners. There are a few things that you can take a look at to limit your risks including:

The margin of profit for that company.

The debts that a company has and how much those debts are.

The return on equity with that company.

The debt to equity ratio. This is a good thing to look up because it will give you an idea of how this particular company spends their money and whether they do so responsibly or not.

How the company has done in the past and whether they are expected to do the same, better, or worse.

What should I be looking for?

So, you may be curious about what things you need to look for to pick out a good company to invest in. You will want to spend some time looking through charts and graphs to see how a particular stock has been doing inside the stock market, but that is only one part of the story. You also need to take a look at the company itself to see if it will maintain that status for the long term. For example, there may be a company who looks good when you go through the charts and graphs, but if they are not good at spending money or keeping their debts down, then they are not the company for you. Some of the different things that you should consider looking at when you are ready to pick out a stock includes:

Who manages the business

This is one of the first things that you should look at when you want to start investing in a company. Who manages the business will help you to figure out how the company is doing now as well as how it will do in the future. Many beginners consider the management of a company not all that important. However, if the current management is not doing well with running the company, even a solid company can go downhill fast.

Now, you need to carefully consider the management of a company before you decide to invest in it. There are a few points that you can consider such as what the return on equity is if the shareholders are still earning a profit each year. If the equity return of the company is five percent or higher, it is usually a safe bet that the company will keep growing and doing well. Also, look and see how the management is doing with others and with each other. Are they getting along and making decisions that are good for the company, or is there are a lot of internal fighting that could ruin the company?

Pick a sector that is doing well

When you are picking out stocks, it is important that you find some that come from a business sector that is also doing well. Depending on how the economy is doing, it is possible that some industries will still do well in a downturn, or at least some industries will do better than the rest. There are also times when the economy is doing well, but one or two industries are not doing as well as the rest of the market.

This is why it is so important to pick out industries that are doing well. You may also want to consider spreading your money out a bit so that you can avoid trouble if one of your industries starts to do poorly. And, while it is best to go with industries that are predicted to do well over a long period of time, if you find that one of your industries is not performing the way that you want, it is easy to sell that stock and try something else.

Growing profits

You also need to look for a company that is making profits. If you see a company that is losing money from the start, then it will be hard for you to get a good return on investment. You also want to make sure that the company is getting bigger profits each year. When the company keeps on growing their profits, it is doing well and has a lot of popularity that is growing as well. This makes it a good investment option for many people. The bigger the profits, the better return on investment you will be able to get.

The size of your company

Some investors want to work with a company that is a little bit smaller. They think that these are easier to work with and that they will be able to monitor that company a little bit better than some of the bigger companies. However, there have been some studies done that show

how smaller companies will actually carry more risks with them compared to investing in some of the bigger companies.

The reason for this is that a lot of the bigger companies have taken their time to become established. They didn't become big overnight, so you know that they will be safe investments. As a beginner who has never worked in the stock market, it is usually better to go with a company that is bigger and more established. After you have learned how to work in the stock market and you understand the types of risks that you want to take, you can choose to go with a smaller company if you would like.

Also, as a beginner, you should make sure that you are avoiding penny stocks. These sometimes are tempting because they are usually really inexpensive to work with. However, these companies are really risky and often they do not need to provide users and investors with financial information even though they are on the exchange. It is likely that you will lose a lot of money if you choose to work with these penny stocks. It is a better idea to stick with one of the main companies that are on the stock market so that you know they are safer options and you are more likely to make money.

Look at the dividend payments

When you look at a company, check and see if they are able to pay out dividends to their investors. Companies that are able to share their profits already are great options for a beginner to work with. This shows that the company is already able to manage their debts while still sharing the profits with the shareholders. It is likely that they will be able to do it again and you will continue to receive these payments in the future.

Also, when you are deciding how much you can make with dividend payments, you should go with a company that is able to pay you at least two percent. This is a good sign that the company is pretty steady and that you will be able to make a decent amount of money each year. If you can find one that is higher than the two percent, then you are able to make even more in profits.

Manageable debt

While you are taking a look at some of these companies to invest in, you should take a look at the debts that they have. The company doesn't necessarily need to be completely debt free, but they need to have a good balance between the amount of debt that they take on and the amount of profit that they are able to bring out.

There are some good debts that a company will have, especially if they are just starting out or if they have recently undergone an expansion. They may have some debts for their buildings, for their equipment and so much more. You are not likely to find a company that doesn't have any debt, but you should look for one that has kept their debt manageable for the profits that they make each year. If you are looking for a company and they have so much debt that they are barely able to cover it each month, then it is best to go with someone else. In this case, it is unlikely that they will be able to keep managing that debt and you will lose money.

Go with liquid stocks

And finally, another thing that you can consider when you are looking at stocks to invest in is how liquid those stocks are. Liquid stocks are good because these are the ones that you will easily be able to find sellers and buyers for. If you go with a stock that is not liquid, you may find that it is really hard to sell that stock later on when you want to leave the market. Most stocks will have some kind of liquidity with them, but the more liquid the stock is considered, the easier it is for you to sell it when you would like.

Try to find a stock that has a happy medium. You want it to be at a good price, so you do not want the demand for that stock to be too high. If the demand is too high, it will be too expensive to get ahold of it to start. But the demand needs to be high enough that when you are ready to leave the market, no matter what that reason is, you will be able to find someone who is willing to purchase the stocks from you.

There are a lot of things that you will need to consider when it comes to picking out the right stocks for your needs. You should do your research to figure out who is managing the company, how they are doing with their profits and their debts, and find stocks that will be easy to sell if you decide to leave the market. When you are able to do this, you are sure to find some good and secure stocks that will help you to make a good profit.

# Chapter 4: Measurements

Price/Earnings Ratio (PER)

It describes the relationship between the current price of the share and the annual profit per share. The P / E ratio is a prominent tool for assessing the profitability and development of a company in comparison to others, also known as the price-earnings ratio (PER).

The P / E ratio is straightforward to calculate: the current share price is divided by the earnings per share. The P / E ratio indicates how many times the profit attributable to stock is currently being valued. In other words, it describes the number of years in which the company would have earned its market value if profits were constant.

But where does the winning number come from? The P / E ratio is usually based on the estimated profit for the current or the next year. This is an attempt to do justice to the expected profit development because the information from the current period is already anticipated in the prices on the stock exchange. The old stock market saying, "The future is traded on the stock exchange," also applies to the P / E analysis.

Shortcomings of the P/E ratio

The Price equity ratio is one of the frequently used indicators for stock valuation. However, its application is more complicated than the formula given above suggests.

Profits cannot simply be carried forward into the future. Cyclical fluctuations have to be taken into account as well as effects of internal changes as well as changes in competition, consumer behavior, interest rate developments, and product life cycles, etc. Unpredictable variables such as weather and political decisions also play a role in some industries.

One-off, extraordinary income, and expenses are to be ignored, as are temporary fluctuations in the tax rate.

If the estimate is uncertain, risk deductions must be made. In contrast, if the growth prospects are sure, a P / E premium is possible.

Profits can be manipulated within certain limits by creating and releasing hidden reserves and changing payment terms. An additional analysis of the cash flow can provide information about this.

The price equity ratio describes the current earnings situation of the company, not the future one. A company that makes little profit today because a lot of money goes into product development may have a better future perspective than a similar company that makes more profit but neglects product development.

Stock corporations report different profit indicators in press releases, for example, with or without non-group profit shares. Sometimes only earnings before taxes or before taxes and interest are mentioned. Earnings per share after deduction of interest expenses, taxes, and non-group profit shares are relevant for the P / E ratio.

You also need to consider whether the current stock price was used in the calculation or average.

Debt Equity Ratio

In the world of corporate finance, Debt to Equity Ratio is an important metric. The Debt to Equity Ratio is a tool used to appraise the financial leverage of a company by ascertaining the proportion of shareholders' equity and debt used to finance assets. The ratio makes a comparison between the future obligations of a company relative to the equity it has.

The general formula for calculating the debt to equity ratio is

Total Debt / Total Equity. However, depending on the type of debt and definition, there are other formulas:

Long Term Debt / Total Equity

Total Liabilities / Total Equity

High Debt to Equity ratio means that a higher percentage of financing comes from debts and a low rate from stakeholders' Equity. Therefore, the cash flow of a company might not be enough to cater for its debts. This is viewed by a creditor as risky because investors' failure to fund the company might be a result of the company underperforming. A low Debt to Equity ratio means that more financing comes from stakeholders' equity. However, this can be indicative of a company's failure to maximize profits through financial leveraging.

There's a significant increase in the potential to generate earnings if a lot of debt is used in financing the growth of a company. There is a considerable risk to the shareholders if there is a higher leverage ratio. Share values will decline in cases where debt financing costs more than the income generated, but if the leverage increases earnings greater than the interest paid on debts, the shareholders will benefit.

Debt to Equity ratio is often focused on long term debt because of the risk associated with long term liabilities. However, investors can improve the Debt to Equity ratio by incorporating short term leverage ratios, profit performance, and growth expectations.

Return on Equity

Return on Equity (ROE) measures the profitability of a business relative to its Equity. It calculates how much profit a company makes per unit of shareholders' Equity. ROE is considered as a measure of how adequately administration is utilizing the assets of a company to generate revenue or profits. A company with a rising ROE is one with an increasing ability to generate income without requiring much capital.

ROE is calculated with the formula:

ROE = Net Income / Shareholders' Equity. The ROE can be calculated only if the values of the Net income and equity are positive.

According to DuPont ROE is equal to the product of profit margin, asset turnover and financial leverage of the company, given by the formula: ROE = (Net Income/Sales) * (Sales/Total Assets) * (Total Assets/Shareholders' Equity)

ROE values can go up in instances where the equity of shareholders' goes down or in cases where there are high levels of debts. It should be noted that write-downs and share buybacks can artificially increase ROE values. Just like with the Debt-Equity ratio, making comparisons of ROE is meaningful within the context of companies in the same industry; therefore, a good or bad ROE can be determined based on the average ROE of the companies.

It's a powerful tool investors use to track performance as it measures how efficiently the shareholders' money is being managed. It is critical to first compare certain industrial sectors to the overall market. Then compare individual companies' ROE with the market and then other companies in the industry.

Share buybacks can alter the value of ROE; for instance, when shares are repurchased by the company, the number of outstanding shares reduces, thereby increasing the value of the ROE.

Price to Book Ratio

The Price to Book ratio is used to juxtapose the current market price of a company against its book value. This is done by dividing the current share price by the book value per share. As a tool for financial valuation, it evaluates the value of a company's stock through a comparison of the price of outstanding shares against its net assets. This ratio differentiates between the market value of a company and its book value. The current stock value of all outstanding shares of a company is its market price. The book value is always the net assets of the company.

The formula for calculating the Price to Book ratio is:

Price to Book Ratio = Market Price per Share /.Book Value per Share

For example, if an investor is interested in investing in a company. The said company has 100,000 outstanding shares traded at $2.5 per share, and the book value of the company is $150,000. The Price to Book Ratio is calculated thus:

Price to Book Ratio = $2.5 / $1.5 = 1.67

This is an indicator that the company's stock cost 1.67 times the book value.

A company with a Price to Book ratio greater than 1 indicates that investors are willing to pay more for the company than the net worth of its assets, while a ratio lower than one means the company is undervalued and stocks are being sold at a value lesser than the worth of its assets.

The value of 3 is the benchmark for a Price to Book value according to value investors. Investors, however, are more inclined to invest in companies with a Price to Book Ratio less than one due to a potentiality of an undervalued stock. The ratio helps an investor to know whether they are investing too much in a company on the brink of bankruptcy.

Price to Book ratio is especially useful if a company has negative earnings or inconsistent earnings as other metrics might not give a clear view of the company's true value and when evaluating a company with a significant amount of intangible assets. Intangible assets come in various forms, such as patents and intellectual properties. The ratio that becomes even more useful when combined with the Return on Equity ratio.

Price to Book ratio comparisons may not be comparable for companies with different countries of operations, and also, the ratio doesn't provide out rightly any information on the company's ability to generate profit for stakeholders.

Price to Earnings to Growth Ratio

Price to Earnings to Growth Ratio determines the value of the stock while taking into account the company's expected earnings growth. This ratio is used as a way of enhancing the Price to Earnings ratio through the factoring of expected earnings growth, and it's considered as the true indicator of the true value of a stock. It builds on the Price to Earnings ratio through the factoring of growth into the equation. This provides a significant element to stock valuation as equity investments reflect a financial interest in the future earnings of a company.

The formula for calculating the Price to Earnings Ratio (PEG) is given as:

Price to Earnings to Growth Ratio = (Price / Earnings per Share) / (Earnings per Share Growth)

For example: If a company has a price to earnings ratio of 12 and a growth rate of 8, the PEG is 1.5. Choosing a growth rate for PEG is not quite straightforward. A stock might have a growth rate of 25%, but it is projected that the growth rate will plummet to 15% at some future period. In this case, you can choose any of them either, or an average of both.

We have two types of PEG: Forward and Trailing. The Forward PEG utilizes a future growth, while the Trailing PEG uses a trailing growth based on some past growth rate such as that of the previous fiscal year. PEG can be calculated for a period of time longer than five years, but as they stretch forward, predictions become less accurate.

A low PEG ratio represents an undervaluation of stocks. A PEG ratio of 1 represents a reasonably valued stock at the expected growth. A negative PEG represents a drop in future earnings or negative earnings in the present.

If you choose between two stocks from the same business firms, then you might want to look at their PEG ratios and make your decision. For example, Company Y's stock may sell for ten times its earnings, whereas Company Z's stock may trade 12 times its earnings. If you just look at the P / E ratio, then the more attractive alternative might seem to be Company Y. Company Y, however, has a projected growth rate of 11% per year in earnings over five years, while Company Z's earnings have a projected growth rate of 17% per annum over the same period. Here is what their calculations for the PEG ratio:

Y PEG = 10/ 11 = 0.91

Z PEG = 12 /17 = 0.71

This points out that when taking growth into account, company Z would be more preferred because it is being traded at a discounted value compared to its actual value.

Understanding these ratios will go a long way to determine how well a stock is performing, how it will perform, and importantly when to enter the market, as we will see. Furthermore, when looking for trading platforms, ensure they have these indicators available on them alongside technical indicators and other related research tools.

# Chapter 5: An Understanding Of Stocks

Stocks are a type of equity investment that reflects the percentage of a company that you own which is measured in shares. When you own shares of a company, you own a part of the company, and you therefore have the right to claim part of the company's assets and earnings. The more stocks you own in a company, the greater your ownership stake in the said company becomes. Corporations usually issue shares for purchase when they need to raise money, and this is accomplished through an IPO (Initial Public Offering).

During an IPO, companies price shares according to their market value and the number of shares being sold. Although the shares you buy from a company are traded on an exchange (like the New York Stock Exchange), the company utilizes the money received to grow its business. You, as the investor or trader, can buy and sell the company's stock continually on an exchange or keep it all for yourself; the company receives nothing because they only get funds from the IPO.

A long time ago, if you bought shares of a company, you were given a paper stock certificate as a way to verify your ownership of those shares. Unlike the past, your brokerage firm records the shares you buy in an electronic database. Due to the tricky nature of stock market investing you should take all of your investments seriously and treat them each as a business.

Mastering stock market investment basics should be your priority before buying your first shares. Although this won't make you a seasoned investor overnight, it will set you on the right path to becoming one. Knowledge is power, and with the right skills you'll soon be able to invest in the stock market with confidence.

Company Ownership

When you buy shares in a company, you become a shareholder, meaning you are one of the company's many owners, and to a certain extent you can claim everything owned by the company. Technically, this means that you own a certain percentage of the company's trademark, furniture, profits, contracts, etc, depending on the number of shares you own.

As a public company's shareholder, you get one vote for every share you buy. This means that you do not get to engage in the company's daily decision-making process regarding how the business is run. However, you can use your votes during the company's annual meetings to elect members of the board of directors. For instance, if you own shares of Google, you cannot dictate to the CEO how you think the firm should be run, though it is the role of the company's management to increase the value of your shares as well as that of the other shareholder's shares.

Theoretically, you, the shareholder, have the voting right to remove the management if they are not able to raise the value of your stock. However, this cannot happen in reality, because the stock owned by shareholders is not enough to give them the power to influence any major decisions within the firm; it is the entrepreneurs worth billions and large institutional investors that have this power.

As an ordinary shareholder, it is not a big deal if you cannot influence major decisions in a company in which you own shares. What is important is that your money is working for you, in addition to having rights to part of the firm's assets and profits. You definitely can be paid your share of the profits as dividends. The amount of profits you receive is directly related to the number of shares you own in the company: the more shares you own, the more the profits and vice versa. You can only claim your rights to the company's property in the case that it goes bankrupt. The way it usually works is that all the creditors get paid first, after which you get paid what remains.

You should note that stock ownership is as important as your claim on the firm's earnings and assets; the two go hand in hand. Moreover, your liability is limited, which means that if the company is in debt you are not liable. However, this is not the case with partnerships, where shareholders or partners are responsible for the company's debts.

Irrespective of what might happen, the only thing you can lose in the stock market is your investment, which are your shares. Your personal assets remain yours.

Debt versus Equity

You might be wondering why a company would sell its stock to hundreds or thousands of people when the founders could keep all the earnings for themselves. Well, companies usually need to raise some money at one point or another. They can achieve this through debt financing that entails borrowing money through bond issuance or from a bank, and equity financing that entails stock issuance.

Unlike debt financing, equity financing has more pros for the company. For instance, the company neither pays back the funds raised nor offers interest to the buyers. The shareholders, who are the stock buyers, only have to hope that one day their shares would be worth more than their buying price. Private companies usually issue their first sale of shares through an initial public offering, an IPO.

It is essential for you as a beginner to understand the differences between the equity and debt financing of companies. When you invest in debt through purchasing bonds, you can be sure that you will get back your money and the interest earned over the duration of the investment. On the other hand, with an equity investment, you become one of the business owners, a shareholder; hence, you bear all the benefits, losses, and risks of the company.

When you become a shareholder in a company, you are similar to being a small business owner who is not guaranteed any returns on their investments. Unlike the company's creditors, you, the shareholder, has less of a claim on the firm's assets. In the case the company liquidates or declares bankruptcy, the most absolute priorities first comes into play before you. This means that you are only paid after all the bondholders and banks, who are the firm's creditors, are paid their dues.

Despite the fact that the shareholders lose all of their investments if the company is not successful, you can earn a lot of money from your equity investment if the company is successful.

Stocks and Risk

When it comes to stock market investing, you should know that there are no guarantees. Although some companies can pay you dividends, several others will not. Furthermore, even though some firms have a history of paying their shareholder's dividends, they have no obligation to continue doing the same in the future. With no dividends, you can only make money from your shares if their value appreciates over time. However, if the company goes bankrupt, your investment becomes valueless.

On the flip side, if you put your money in investments with high risks, you stand the chance of getting higher returns on your investment. This explains why stocks have always performed better than bonds and saving accounts. Historically, investments in stocks have had up to 10% to 12% returns over a long duration.

Types Of Stock

Most people just assume that all stocks are the same. You will be surprised to learn that there are different types of stock. There are two major types of stock, common stock and preferred stock, with the former giving shareholders voting rights without any dividend payment guarantees and the latter offering shareholders no voting rights with a dividend payment guarantee.

Common Stock

This is the most common type of stock in the investment market. In fact, when you hear people talking of stock, this is what they are normally referring to because most stocks are sold in this form. The common stock shares reflect your ownership of a company and dividend claims come in the form of profits. For every single vote per stock you get as an investor, you get the right to elect the board members who ensure that the company's management makes the right decisions all the time.

Unlike many other investments, you can earn higher returns on your capital growth by investing in common stock over prolonged periods. The cost of you getting higher returns lies in the high risk associated with common stock investments. As mentioned before, you are also not paid until all the creditors receive their dues in the case of a bankruptcy.

Preferred Stock

Although preferred and common stock reflect your ownership of a company to some degree, the former does not come with voting rights, depending on the firm in question. When you invest in preferred stock shares, you are guaranteed dividends depending on the kind of preferred stock. This is unlike the common stock with no guaranteed variable dividends. Moreover, if you own preferred shares in a company, you are paid before the common stock shareholders are paid, but of course after the creditors receive their dues in the case of a bankruptcy.

However, in the case the company needs to raise a premium, they would buy your preferred shares because they are callable. According to certain people, preferred stock is more of a debt than an equity. You can consider preferred stock to exist between common stock and bonds.

Distinct Stock Classes

Although stocks are mainly categorized as common or preferred, companies can tailor the distinct stock classes as they want. A company can do this if they want only a specific group to own voting rights. Therefore, each of the distinct stock classes is given a unique voting right. For instance, a specific class of stock entailing the majority of shareholders could be given a single voting right per share, whereas another class of a select shareholder group could be given 10 voting rights per share.

The distinct stock classes are usually grouped into classes ranging from Class A to Z, depending on the number of classes. The BRK ticker, Berkshire Hathaway has a couple of stock classes only. In order to create a distinct form, its class letter is placed after the ticker symbol, like "BRK.A, BRK.B" or "BRKa, BRKb".

## Chapter 6: What Options Do I Have For Stock Market Investing?

There are quite a few options that you will be able to choose when you are ready to invest in the stock market. You will need to learn how to narrow down the niche and the industry that you want to work in to make things a little bit easier. While it is important to diversify your portfolio at some point, it is best for a new investor to keep things small.

The strategy that you choose to help you start investing will depend on a number of factors. Sometimes it depends on the money that you have to start with and how much you want to make. Sometimes it depends on the amount of risk involved or the research that you have done on the topic. But even when you have a good plan with lots of research, there are reasons why you should be skeptical and take your time with everything. In this chapter, we will talk about some of the options and even some of the niches that you can choose to help you invest in the right stocks for you.

Dividend Stocks

The first strategy that you can choose is to work with dividend stocks, and it works the best if you would like to pick out a long-term investment. Dividend stocks may not make you rich overnight, but it will help you to earn a lot of money consistently over many years. When going with dividend stocks, you want to make sure that you are picking stocks from companies that are doing well now and are projected to do well in the future. There are quite a few companies who will work out well for this, and if you pick the right one, you will be able to enjoy a percentage of the profits from that company each quarter for as long as you hold the stocks.

Now, it is important to realize that not all stocks that are available on the exchange will work with dividends. This means that you need to check with each company before deciding to use them for this process. Screening companies is a good idea as well because this will help you to figure out which companies will actually give you a dividend each quarter (if the company doesn't make a profit, they are not able to provide their shareholders with any dividends). Each company that trades on the stock exchange will need to put out financial statements. Make sure to utilize these to help you make good decisions.

As you go through your research, you should be able to come up with a list of companies that pay their shareholders a decent dividend. But you do not want to start out with too many companies, so it is now time to narrow the list down a little bit to find those that meet all your criteria. Some of the things that you should look into with each company that you are interested in will include:

Look to see if the company has had a steady history of paying out their dividends. It is not a good thing if there is a lot of missed dividend payments because this could show that there are some major issues with the company. It is best to go through their history as far as possible to see how consistent the dividend payments are.

The next thing to look for is how high the return on equity is for this company. To make sure that you are picking out a good company, you need to look over the past five years and see a return on equity of at least fifteen percent if not higher.

Each share that you are considering needs to have rising earnings and sales over time. If the shares are going down, then you know that you will lose money if you go with this stock.

The dividends that are provided to the shareholders need to grow as well. This means that you will earn more money over time, instead of getting the exact same amount every year. A good company will see a growth in their dividends of at least five percent over ten years.

Take a look at the list of companies that you are interested in and check to see if they meet some of the requirements above. If they do, then they are a great option to go with, and you should consider investing your money in them.

Foreign stock investing

Another option that you can choose to go with is the foreign stock investing. This is an option that most beginners do not stick with because it is hard to follow what is going on in a foreign market. This means that if you want to go into this type of market, you need to do some extra research and pay special attention to what is going on in other countries. If you do this process correctly, there are a lot of companies overseas that are promising and can bring in more money than you can get in your own country. However, it is important to realize that some risks come with working with foreign stock investing.

There are actually a few benefits that you can enjoy when it comes to investing in foreign stocks. Some of the benefits that you will enjoy with these stock options include:

The stocks that are available in foreign markets will provide you with some new investment opportunities. Based on your goals for investing, it sometimes is a little hard to find a company that you want to invest in, especially if you limit yourself to your own country. You may find that it is easier to find the right investments when you look in other markets.

Foreign stocks can be a good option for those who are looking for new ways to diversify their portfolios. This can help you to spread out some of your risks, so consider investing your money into a variety of companies, even if you are looking at foreign markets.

While these benefits are really tempting for a beginner who wants to find lucrative companies to invest in, it is important to remember that working in a foreign market actually provides a much higher risk than working in the stock exchange in your market. Even if the company looks like a good and safe investment, it is important to take into account the exchange rate. Depending on which market you go into and the amount of dividend that you expect to make, the cost of exchanging the currency over to USD may take all your profits, which makes the risk of investing in these markets higher than before.

The market conditions are often going to be very different in another country compared to what is going on in your country. For example, the United States may be seeing an upturn in their economy while other countries deal with economies that are shaky. It does not matter what is going on in your home country; what matters is what is going on in whatever country you would like to invest in. This can be good news if the economy in your home country is doing poorly, but it is still something to be aware of.

While there is a lot of potential to make a high profit when you decide to invest in a foreign market, it is very risky, and that is why a lot of beginners choose to not go with this option at all. It may be a good idea to find a good broker and get some help if you decide to go with this as your investment option.

Penny stocks

Penny stocks are an option for investing that some people like to work with, but you have to realize that these are really risky. Beginners like these stocks because they are less expensive than some of the bigger names that are on the stock exchange. If you do not have a lot of money to get started with for this investment, the penny stocks can be a good option for you to go with because you may be better able to afford them.

It is important to realize that not all the companies on the penny stock exchange are reputable. These companies do not need to disclose financial information, and they do not need to meet the same requirements thatcompanies on the stock exchange need to. While there are some companies who will sell shares on this exchange to help them out while they are trying to meet the requirements of the stock exchange (and these are often really good companies to consider because their prices will go up), there are also a lot of failing companies that are working as penny stocks.

This can make it hard to know who you should work with. These penny stocks are really risky, and it is not always the best idea for a beginner to get into this market. Sometimes the value of the stock is hard to figure out, and even a little bit of negative movement can cause a big impact on your investment. Many times these companies are able to hide information from you, and you can lose out your whole investment in no time. These stocks are really volatile as well, which makes it harder to watch the market and make good decisions.

If you are a beginner and you are interested in checking out penny stocks and learning how they work, then you need to be careful and fully aware of all the risks that come with it. Some of the guidelines that you can consider following when you want to get into penny stocks and still see a return on your investment include:

Pay attention to some of the warnings that you see. There are some regulators on this market, and if they are sending out some warnings about a particular company, it is worth your time to pay attention.

Don't always believe what you see. These companies are not held up to the same standards as companies on the stock exchange are. Do your own research and learn as much about the company as possible.

Learn some more about how penny stocks work. We talked briefly about them, but it is so important to take a look at these stocks and learn more about them before you enter the market.

Some companies will offer penny stocks, but they are not going to provide you with a lot of information. The less information that is present in a company, the bigger the risk there is to invest in them. Double check that a company is as honest as possible with their information, especially financial information, before you decide to invest.

These are some of the main options that you can work with when you are ready to invest your money in the stock market. Make sure to look through each category and decide which one is the best for your needs.

# Chapter 7: Common Terms

An investor needs to understand some basic terms that are used regularly in the stock market if they want to invest. It is only when you understand these terms well that you can make the right decisions. These terms will help you understand how the stock market operates. You will also understand what terms you need to look for when you trade in the market.

## Ask

When you trade-in stocks, you will need to place a bid on a stock that you want to purchase. The price that you place on a share is called the ask. This price should be close to what the seller requests. This price is what you believe is the best bid that you can make on the stock. You need to perform due diligence and analysis before you place the ask on a stock. It is only when you understand the company well and look at the price movement of the stock that you can place a bid on that stock. Some investors choose to place lower ask prices because they believe that the price of the stock will fall in the future. Other investors place high ask values under the pretext that there will be an increase in the price. One can only make these assumptions after performing a thorough analysis of the stock.

Bearish Reversal

The bearish reversal is a term that is assigned to the market. This situation will occur when the price of the stock today is lower than the price of the stock when the market closed yesterday. This shows that there is a downward trend in the price of the stock. When numerous investors sell their stocks, the value of the stock will reduce. If you have invested in some bad stocks, you will lose money. If the stock continues to follow this pattern, you cannot understand the trend of that stock. The stock price can either move upwards or downwards, depending on the market. It is always a good idea to wait and see how the price moves before you choose to sell or hold your stocks. So, wait for the price to stabilize before you make your decision. If you think the stock will continue to follow this trend, you should sell the stock immediately.

## Bid

The bid refers to the price at which the stocks are sold in the market.

## Broker

Most people who want to invest in the stock market cannot put in too much effort. They do not have the time to study the market and make the right investment. This is when they will turn to a broker. A broker is someone who will help you trade your stocks. When you want to trade in the stock market, you need to be a member of the stock exchange. Otherwise, you are not allowed to trade in the market. To become a member, you will need to know the steps to follow, and a broker can help you understand the same.

Brokers are always a part of companies that are members of the stock exchange.

Some brokers also choose to go out on their own, but they will be members of the stock exchange. Since the broker only follows the market, they know exactly what stock you should look at. They can advise you about the investments you need to make based on the analysis they perform and your risk tolerance. The final decision, however, is yours. If you do not want to trust your broker fully, you can perform some analysis to assess whether the stock is indeed good to invest in. Depending on how much money you have, you can choose to hire a part-time or full-time broker. A full-time broker is someone who will constantly work on your investment profile. The broker will invest in the right stocks to ensure that you will make a profit. This broker will look at the trends of the market and alert you if there is a good deal that they come across. A part-time broker is someone who will only buy and sell your stocks. He will not give you advice or spend time to help to maximize your profits. The former will charge you more since he spends all his time on investing for you. We will look at the different types of brokers later in the book. Always perform research and hire a broker who is both trustworthy and reliable. Ask people you know about a broker they will recommend. You can also read the testimonials to see which broker you should approach. These testimonials are proof of who you can and cannot trust.

Bullish Reversal

A bullish reversal, like the bearish reversal, refers to a change in the price of the stock. It is the exact opposite of the bearish reversal. When the price of stock constantly moves upward, the stock is said to follow a bullish trend. A bullish trend occurs when the lowest price of the stock on the previous day, and the price of the stock on the current day are greater than the closing price of the stock on the previous day. This means that the price of the stock will continue to increase, and the trend will help you realize if you are investing to make a profit or a loss. This trend will occur only when there are more buyers than sellers in the market, and the demand is greater than the supply. You should always follow this trend and sell the stocks immediately if you wish to make a profit. The price of the stock will continue to rise, which will make it easier for you to dispose of the stocks you have. You need to make quick decisions since you cannot expect the price of the stock to remain the same. The price of the stock is volatile, which means that it can change within a fraction of a second. An inexperienced hand will find it hard to judge the situation and make the right decision. It will be difficult for you to assess how the price of the stock will move.

## Commission

You must pay the broker some commission for the services that he or she provides. This broker will help you buy and sell stocks, and may also give you some suggestions. For this, they will charge you a commission. The amount that is deducted from your profit does not go only to the broker. Some of the commission will go to the company as well. The commission charged will vary from one company to another. You should pick the company that charges the lowest rate. If you do not want to compromise on quality and are willing to spend more, you can choose a good broker. You must assess the company to see if it is good and whether the brokers in that company are good at what they do. You can also request the company to assign you to a broker who has a good reputation.

Day Trading

Day trading is a very common term used in the stock market. This is a trading strategy that is commonly used by investors. Day trading in stocks refers to when a trader buys and sells stocks on the same day to make a profit from the differences between the buying and selling prices. The investor will look for a way to purchase the stocks when the market opens. The price of the stock when the market opens is low. The trader will then sell the stock during the day when the prices continue to rise. Traders should set buy, hold, and sell triggers to help them understand how they should work with the stock. It is difficult for an amateur to set the limits since they do not have enough experience with trading. Stocks do not necessarily have to follow a predictable pattern, and you need to understand the stock fully and analyze the movements. The prices of some stocks will rise during the first few hours of the day and will fall during the day. Some stocks may also follow the opposite pattern. Stocks are traded differently in different countries, and you should understand the differences before you begin trading in different countries.

Due Diligence

You must perform due diligence before you choose to invest in any stock in the market. You will come across this term whenever you read articles about stock investing. You need to understand the stock and the company before you invest your money in the company. You should ensure that you obtain this information from reliable sources, so you do not have to risk your funds. Assess all the data that you have collected it, and analyze that data to verify if the stock that you wish to invest in is worthy of your money. Make these decisions based on trends. Always study the data carefully. This will help you understand if you can profit from investing in the stock. You will find information about the stock on the Internet, and you can use that information to conduct the analysis. Never invest in stock only because other people have invested in that stock. People tend to buy a stock too much using some information shared by the management.

## Hedge

You can purchase a futures contract or sell it as a temporary substitute for any cash market. You can sell or purchase this contract at a later date. This transaction will involve a position in both the futures market and the cash market. This position will need to be maintained at the same time.

Limit Order

You should always place a limit order on your stock, so you know when to sell it. When the price of the stock hits the limit order, you need to sell the stock. If you use a broker, you can instruct them to sell the stock at the limit order. Make sure that you let the broker know that he should never sell the stock at a price that is lower than the limit order. You will have calculated your profit margin based on the limit order, and you must ensure that you stick to that percentage gain. If you are unsure of how to set this price, you can use different applications or software to do this for you. If you want to use online trading techniques, you can set the limit order on the application. When the price of the stock reaches the limit order, the application will sell the stock at that rate. You do not have to track the price constantly.

## Portfolio

Your investment sheet called the portfolio. Your portfolio holds the information about all the investments you make and will include details about the stocks you hold, the ones you sold, stock value, number, the price at which the stock was bought, profit made, unrealized profits, and more. You must maintain these details and ensure that you understand this information well. You can assess your investment trend using this investment portfolio. If you practice the day trading strategy, you need to check the portfolio, so you assess whether you have traded in the right stocks or not. When you check your investment portfolio, you can identify the errors you have made. This will give you the option to correct these errors immediately.

Profit Percentage Gain

You, as a trader, must set a profit percentage gain. This percentage will give the broker an idea of where you have pegged the profits. As a trader, you can make a profit if you stick to the profit percentage gain. You can calculate this percentage based on when you buy or sell the stocks and at what price. Every trader has some expectations regarding their investments, and they will decide the stocks they should invest in based on their profit percentage gain.

Stock Split

The stock split refers to how the company has decided to split the stock into numerous stocks to increase the number of stocks it provides. Most companies do this when they notice that their stocks have been bought quickly. When this happens, the company needs to increase its share in the market. The company can then split the stocks to pump in more shares. It is a good thing if this happens, especially if you hold stocks. When you hear the announcement, you will know how many bonus shares are available. This will increase your profit.

Stop Loss Percentage

You will also hear the term stop-loss percentage frequently when you trade. This percentage is a value that you set to determine to what extent you can take a loss. If you set the percentage to 10%, and the value of the stock that you invested in begins to fall by 10%, you should let go of that stock so you can maintain your capital and accept the loss. This is an extremely important percentage that you should bear in mind when it comes to trading in the stock market, and this is especially true for stock traders. Many traders worry that they will incur a loss if they sell a stock without waiting for the price to increase. This is the wrong way to approach the situation. If you wait for the price to increase, you may lose out on an opportunity to make a profit. You may also risk getting your capital stuck in that stock alone. You should instead choose to assume a position from the same place or invest in a better stock. If you use this method, you can ensure that your capital is not locked in a bad investment. Consider the following example: if you buy 100 stocks from a company at $1 each, you will have invested $100 of your capital in that stock. You hope that the price of the stock will increase to $1.05 by the end of the day. You should place a stop-loss percentage of 10$ on that stock if the price drops to lower than what you expected. So, you should set your stop loss amount at $0.90. If the price of the stock falls to that number, you know that you should let go of the stock.

Swing Trading

Swing trading is a term that refers to when you sell a stock when the price reaches your stop loss mark. You will then take a fresh position in the market. The objective behind swinging is to capitalize on the volatility of the stock. When you do this, you can cover any losses that you may make. It is believed that the price of the stock will increase steadily when it hits a low. So, if the stock reaches a low price, you will know that the price will rise again.

Traders prefer to place a stop-loss limit based on how much money they can afford to lose. Never underestimate the value of the stop loss method, and try to put that into practice.

**Volume**

The volume of the stock is the number of shares that you can trade at any point in the market. The volume of stocks in the market will constantly change since the asking price of one individual will match the bid price of the stock. This type of matching will occur at multiple points throughout the day, and the volume will never remain stable. It will fluctuate throughout the day, and no tool or software will help you assess how the volumes will fluctuate. Stock will also have volume fluctuations throughout the day, and the volumes will not stabilize at any point until the price of the stock remains constant because of excess buyers or sellers.

# Chapter 8: The Fundamentals Of Investing

When you choose to invest in the stock market, you will hear the term fundamentals used every day. Executives, investors, and analysts appearing on CNBC or any other news channel will talk about the fundamental of stock. A fund manager will always talk about how some stocks have strong fundamentals. Some traders do claim that there is no need to trust the fundamentals of stock since they do not matter. Before you make the decision, you should understand what fundamentals are. In this chapter, we will look at the fundamentals of stocks.

Stock Fundamentals

Fundamental analysis, in simple terms, is where you will look at any data that will impact the value of a stock. This value can be the actual or perceived value. Fundamental analysis is very different from looking at the trading pattern of the

stock itself. As the name suggests, when you perform the fundamental analysis, you will need to go down to the basics. When you perform fundamental analysis, you will need to create a portrait of the company. To do this, you need to identify the style and industry of the company. You will also need to determine the fundamental value of the shares offered by the company. Once you have this information, you can choose to purchase or sell the stock based on the information you collect. When you perform fundamental analysis, you will need to look at the following fundamentals:
• Understand how the company retains the profits to fund future growth
• Cash flow
• Return on assets
• Conservative gearing
• How sound the management uses the capital to maximize the shareholders' returns or earnings
• Stock Metrics Versus Bond Metrics
• Fundamental Approach
A fundamental analyst will always have a

linear approach when it comes to analyzing the performance of a stock. These analysts will always look at different factors that are believed to affect the performance of the stock. These factors include the following:

- Sector or industry
- Competition
- Structure of the management in the company
- The revenue and income of the company and other factors.

The analyst will also look at the growth of the company. A company makes all this information available to the public. The objective is to identify the stocks and see which prices are correctly or incorrectly adjusted in the market. Let us understand this better using the following analogy. Let us assume that the stock market is like the supermarket. The stocks in a supermarket are the products sold in retail stores. An investor is only looking at the products in these retail stores. A shopper is often unreliable since he does not make calculated purchases every time he enters the store. An investor, on the other hand, will always move through the stores and look for the best deals. When the crowd moves away from the PCs, they will start looking at those products that were ignored by other shoppers.

A fundamental analyst can always take a stab to calculate the value of the PC if it were stripped to its parts like memory cards, keyboard, hard disk, and monitor. These variables are synonymous with the liquidation price or book value of the stock in the market. A fundamental analyst will always look at the quality of the PC before they purchase it. They will need to know if the asset will last or break down. They will also look at the specifications, the warranty documents, and other reviews and reports. In the same way, an equity manager or a fundamental analyst will check the balance sheet and other financial statements of the company to assess the stability of the company. Now, a fundamental analyst should try to understand how the PC performs. They should use different criteria like memory, image resolution, or processing power. These criteria are synonymous with the future dividends and earnings one can make from the shares of the company. You can calculate these based on the income statement provided by the company. A fundamental analyst will put all this data together and calculate the base value or the intrinsic value of the share. If the price of the stock in the market is less than the intrinsic price, a fundamental analyst will buy that stock. In this case, the investor will purchase the PC. Otherwise, they will sell the PC that they own or wait until the price of the PC falls before they purchase more.

Good Fundamentals Do Not Lead to Profits

It is difficult to perform fundamental analysis. This is arguably the source of its appeal. When you do enough work to dig into the financial assets, statements, and other information about the company, you can assess the prospects. You can also learn when the price of the stock was undervalued or overvalued. It is only when you do this that you can identify the mistakes in the market and avoid investing in the wrong shares. It is always a good idea to buy a share based on long-term and intrinsic value. This will protect the investor from making losses because of the fluctuations in the prices of shares. It is important to understand that things are not always so simple. You need to understand that the price of a share will vary at random. This means that you cannot only rely on fundamental analysis to invest in stocks. You do not have to use any complex formulae to calculate the value of the share. Through fundamental analysis, you can identify if the price of a stock is undervalued. This does not necessarily mean that the price will increase in the future. If the stock market is doing well, investors can fool themselves to believe that they can choose the right stocks to make profits. An investor should not rely on luck, especially if the outlook is uncertain, and the market falls. Investors must always know what it is that they need to do.

Technical Analysis versus Fundamental Analysis

Fundamental analysis is very different from technical analysis, and we will look at technical analysis in detail in the next chapter. Fundamental analysis will focus only on the intrinsic value of the stock, while technical analysis will focus on the price and trading history of the stock. You can look at the history by looking at trading signals. You can also use other analytical tools to evaluate the stock. A technical analyst believes that the performance of a stock is always based on past performance. The history can help us predict how the stock will perform in the future. Technical analysis is performed on the basis that the movement of a stock in the market is never random. The belief is that a stock will follow trends and patterns that will repeat over time. To understand this better, let us go back to the example above. A technical analyst will ignore the sale of goods. He will only look at what the crowd chooses to buy or sell. When a technical analyst notices that shoppers are purchasing computers, he will purchase as many PCs as possible and bet that the growing demand will only increase the price of a computer. Before you invest in stocks, you should understand these stocks well. You need to look at the stock from different perspectives to assess if they are the best investment for you. This chapter will list some of the best forms of analysis that you can perform to verify your decisions. These analyses are based on the fundamental and technical analysis covered in the previous chapters.

Performing the Analysis

When you choose to invest in a stock, you are investing in the company. It is for this reason that you need to understand the health of the company financially. You should only invest once you perform this analysis. Make sure that you collect the right documents and information that will enable you to make the correct decisions about investing in any stock.

## Income Statement

You should use the income statement that you receive every month from the company to understand where the company makes its money. The income statement has information about both the operating and non-operating incomes. The company makes an operating income when it sells the products or services that it manufactures or produces. So, it is a direct result of the work that they do, which helps them earn their income. Non-operating income, on the other hand, refers to the amount that the company earns other than selling their products and services. A company can earn a non-operating income by selling some of its possessions like televisions, furniture, etc. If you spot anything unusual in the company's non-operating income, it may indicate a financial crisis. So, investigate before you invest in stock from that company.

## Balance Sheet

A balance sheet is a common financial document that every company must maintain to understand and showcase the health of their company. The balance sheet is used to record every transaction of the company, including its debts, assets, and liabilities. When you go through the balance sheet, you should check if the company has the right assets to balance out the liabilities. If they do not have a balance between the assets and the liabilities, it means that their stocks will not work well in the market. On the other hand, if the company has too many assets and very few liabilities, then it is a good company to invest in. Remember that the companies always disclose their balance sheets every quarter. So, make sure that you go through all of them. Apart from looking at these factors, you should also check for numerous other aspects of the balance sheet. You should look at the earnings growth ratio of the company since that will help you predict if the value or the price of the stock will increase in the                                future.

Next, look at the price to earnings ratio. This ratio will give you an idea of the stock of the company is good. Calculate this ratio based on the current price of the share and divide that figure by the total earnings of the company. This will give you the price to earnings ratio. For example, if the price of the stock is $100 and the earnings per share are $5, then the price to earnings ratio is 20%. The stock is not a great investment since the price to earnings ratio is less than the earnings per share. Remember that the stock is said to be good if the price to earnings ratio is high.

You should also look at the dividends that the company offers its shareholders. A dividend will indicate if the business is worth investing in or not. If the company pays a continuous dividend, at a constant rate, you can consider investing in the stocks         of         that         company.

Let us now look at some of the

fundamental aspects that you should look at in the balance sheet.

**Earnings**

Earnings refer to the income of the company. The company will have some incoming money. This money will be generated due to the company's functioning. You have to look at the inflow of money and see how much they are making. You want the correct value here and must be sure of the amount that is earned quarterly. You have to calculate the earnings per share and see if the value of the company is good. The earnings per share should always be on a higher side.

**Profits**

The next thing to check is the profits of the company. You have to see if there are any debts and the assets that they possess. You have to subtract the two, and the remaining value is the profit or the loss. It is a debt-free company, and then there will be no problem. The company will be quite a good choice to invest in. You have to calculate the net profit, which can be arrived at by using the formula net profit/ revenue earned. If you get a large margin of profit, then it means that the company is being operated optimally, and they are well aware of utilizing their budget. Such a company makes for a good investment choice.

Return on Equity

Return on equity is believed to be the most important thing to account for in a company's reports. You have to calculate it and understand what the company's true value is. Return on equity does not take into consideration the per-share value, which makes it a great tool to use and understand the company's true worth. The return on investment can be calculated by dividing net income by shareholders' equity. That will give you a return on equity, which will tell you whether or not the company is a good choice.

PE Ratio

The PE ratio is better known as the price to earnings ratio. This is to determine whether the share is listed at a good price in the market. It can be calculated by dividing the market value of the share by earnings per share. That will give you an idea of what the price to earnings ratio is. The PE ratio will help you determine the value of the company in terms of its growth and help you understand whether it is a good company to invest with.

Price to Book Value

The price to book value refers to the actual value of the stock as compared to its book value. It can be calculated by dividing the current share price with the book value for share. That will give you a good idea of the price to book value. The ratio will tell you if you are overpaying for the stock and if you need to pay lesser for it.

These form the different things that you must look at and arrive at an appropriate value that you can attach to the company. This value is what you have to use to know the company's worth. You then compare it with the market value and see if the stock has been valued at its true worth. Sometimes, you will stumble across overvalued stocks. These can be risky to invest in as any time their prices may fall, and your investment will be in danger. So, stick to the undervalued stocks. Hold onto these stocks until it is a good time to dispose of them.

Cash Flow Statement

Cashflow statements include information about the total cash that is flowing in and out of the company. The cash flow statement will talk about the different incomes and the expenses of the company. You will understand if the company is doing well using that information. This statement is a great tool to use when you want to understand the financial health of the company. There are a few other legal papers that you should go through to understand the financial health of the company. If you think the company is doing well, then you can invest in it. You must invest in the company only when you go through the technical details.

To complete the fundamental analysis, you should check if the company is managed well by the board. The board members make all the decisions about a company. Since they run the business, you must verify if the business is operating peacefully. You can also check if there are any issues internally. Always stay away from businesses where the members constantly fight and never make a unanimous decision.

As mentioned earlier, fundamental trading will refer to the process of looking at the health of the company. This form of trading will require you to look at how the company is faring financially. You should assess the different assets and liabilities that the company holds and decide if it is the right place to invest. You must perform this analysis in the right manner so you can obtain the desired results. The best way to perform this analysis is to read the quarterly and annual financial reports of the company. This will help you gather a clear idea about the financial health of the company. You will also know what type of company you are going to invest in. There are a few reasons why people choose to use this type of analysis to understand if a stock is performing well in the market. The first is to know if the market is pricing the stocks correctly or not. If the market is not pricing the stocks correctly, you know that there will be a correction methodology applied to the stocks. The stock exchange can also list the price of stocks incorrectly. This will make it hard for you to assess the financial health of the company. If the prices are incorrect, you can choose to invest in a stock that is undervalued. This is a gamble since you do not know if a correction will be applied to that price.

Make sure that you look at the true value of a stock and compare that value with the value in the market. If the prices match, then the stock has been priced correctly in the market. Otherwise, the stock has either been undervalued or overvalued. If

the price is undervalued, it is a good
investment                  opportunity.

# Chapter 9: Investment Tips On Stocks, Forex And Day Trading For Beginners

As an online entrepreneur, one thing you learn is that the competition out there is stiff and massive so when you make the first dollar, you deserve one big thumbs up. Now that you've minted some money online, my next question is, what are you going to do with it? Buy some online merchandise, pay your bills, save it in your bank account, donate it to a good cause, invest it or plain burn it. Whichever you choose, it's still the right choice after all its your money. However, indulge me a little bit and let me show you a different way. I suggest you invest it, why? Because if you invest it, you can still do all the above with your money and some, if not more, of it will still be around to spend when you retire.

First things first, we need to ask and answer each of the following questions:

What is investing?

Who is an investor?

What is an investment?

What do I need to be an investor?

Am I an investor right now?

What should I expect when I invest?

- What is an investment? This is the act of putting money into something, in this case an asset, with the expectation that I will gain something in return.

- Who is an investor? Anyone who takes the risk to investment their money in assets with the sole objective that in the future it will pay back more than what they bought it for. To be an investor you need the financial resources and knowledge on how, where and when to invest.

- What is an asset? An asset is anything that is considered to have economic value.

In other words you can exchange it for cash. Simple examples include your car, house, computer, website e.t.c. Cash is also an asset.

- What is a liability? In the context of business, a liability is any obligation owed to someone else. Simple example includes a loan, unpaid bills etc.

- What is capital? These are the resources required in a business to generate revenue or wealth. Simple examples include money, tools and equipment, premises etc.

- What is a share? A share is a single unit of capital. Assuming you have company whose capital is worth $1,000 which in this case is 100% of the capital. A share in that company is worth $1,000/100 = $10.

- Who is a shareholder? An individual or legal entity that owns shares in a company. If you own 50% of the company, your shareholding is (50/100 x 1000) x $10 = $500.

- What is a dividend? This is the portion of a company's profits that is paid to the shareholders. Assuming Company, A made $100,000 in profits and it is decided that each shareholder will receive $1 per share then if you own 50% of the company you will get $50.

- What is interest? This is the compensation paid for using someone else' assets or financial resources. Interest rate is usually calculated in percentage.

The one rule of investing you need to know is that there is always a risk involved, you could make or lose money when investing. However, an investor's job is to mitigate the risk involved and ensure that the chances of making a loss are reduced and those of making money increased.

What are the major investment vehicles available to the layman or beginner investor?

- Stocks or Shares - This is where you buy a part of an existing company, private or public. The return in this class of investment is dividends and capital growth when the stock price goes up or there is a share split or a bonus. These can be purchased at the stock exchange either on the day to day market trading but the best time to enter this market as beginner is when a public company is offering an IPO (Initial Public Offer).

- Collective Investment Funds - In funds, many individual investors pool their money together into a pool fund which the fund manager uses to invest in one or many types of investments like stocks and real estate local and/or off shore on their behalf and also manages the investment portfolio on a day to day basis. The gains made from this portfolio is then divided among the members of the fund depending on how much each has invested into the fund. The biggest benefit in this group is that one gets to invest and benefit from assets, e.g. blue chip counters, that you would not afford if you went into it as an individual.

- Business - Business is the activity of making money or any activity carried out with the main goal being to make a profit. It could be the sale of tangible goods or provision of services. In this case you invest your money in the company that sells the goods and services and in return you get dividends as a shareholder. This is always a good place to start your journey to becoming an investor. There is enough money from the business to start building up an investment portfolio slowly and if you make a mistake and lose money you have a fall back.

- Foreign Exchange or Forex - How would you like to buy currency when is cheap and sell it again when its more expensive. for example, if the USD is worth 0.9CAD today, you can buy some and a sell it after a few days or weeks when it's worth say 1.1CAD thereby making 0.2CAD per dollar. Suppose you'd invested like a 1,000CAD you'd have made like 100CAD all in one transaction.

Remember, an asset brings income which means the house you live in is not an asset, though your banker might tell you otherwise. However, if you buy a house and rent it out, it becomes an asset. The opposite of asset is liability, so as an investor you should always work towards increasing assets and reducing liabilities. That way your gains increase every day else you'll be losing money if liabilities are going up and assets down.

Are you an Investor, a Business Owner, an Employee or Self Employed? The investor earns income from his investments, business owner from his businesses, employee a salary working for the business owner, self-employed from specialized skills or services to the business owner and investor.

These four individuals' ways by which income is earned are part of the Cash Flow Quadrant as explained by author/investor Robert Kiyosaki of Rich Dad Poor Dad fame. The Cash Flow Quadrant and many more investor self-help material available at the Tuwaze Duka. (Duka means 'a shop' in Swahili)

I suggest you start by setting some goals at the beginning of the investment journey and then maintain a diary on the investment transactions and decisions you make every day. After several months you can compare and analyze them against the achievements you will have made after several months.

Stock Exchange For Beginners

Before I start, I ought to point out that these won't be like any other pages 'for beginners' that you have ever seen. Here's why ...

I have been fascinated by investments since I was in my teens. Most teenagers read the sports pages, I read the financial pages. I bought my first shares aged 18. Into adulthood and I became a financial adviser at the grand old age of 24. I have sat and passed numerous financial exams and several investment specific professional qualifications.

I have read dozens of books about stock picking, economics, finance, politics, business, marketing, investment gurus and their autobiographies. In short, I am now past 30 and have spent the better part of my thinking life interested in investments.

I have been involved in a UK based share club and did much of the club's analysis. Aged 23/24 I was involved in managing a portfolio of close to £100,000. I have read hundreds of company reports, annual and interim. I have also looked at hundreds, if not thousands of graphs. Still, to this day, I read about investment markets for perhaps 10 to 15 hours each week.

Again, back in my early 20's, I used to assist a close friend, alas now departed, with his investment holdings and decisions - his portfolio had over 100 UK holdings and he was worth several million pounds.

The point I am getting to here is a simple one. No matter how much you study and work, the investment markets are huge and have so many variations that no one person will ever master them all.

I have friends and clients that work as economists, and really don't understand investments. I have friends that work in Investment banking that categorically do not understand investments.

In fact, as far as I can tell, investment bankers are about the last people on earth that you would want to take investment advice from. They usually have an MBA and a good degree and are very smart people, but generally, the only bit of the financial world that they understand is the area in which they work or have worked in previously.

They can analyze the water industry or whatever specialization it is that they do, but ask them what they would buy if they were to invest their own money now and they have no clue. I can think of a couple I have met whose deep insight into money management goes as far as 'I put it in the bank'.

Geez! And these guys are the smart ones! Heaven help us all!

I could have asked a car mechanic, hairdresser or bricklayer and received better financial advice than that.

So, here's the rub ... There are very few people on earth that can accurately predict which way the stock market or any other investment is going to behave in the short, medium or long term. Very few people indeed. I don't claim to be one of them.

The few people that can do this, charge a fortune for their advice or do not actually give any advice, they operate for themselves only. This makes some sense. Do Warren Buffett or George Soros offer advice to individuals? No they do not, not at any price.

The people that do have the kind of grasp over market movements that I am writing of usually belong to the 'technical' school of thought. This means that they follow a price, moving averages, indicators, market action in a rather mechanical way, but the art comes in how they interpret those charts!

I don't have a number for this, what I am about to say next is pure speculation, but as wild as it will seem, I would not be surprised if it is actually correct. I imagine that of all the hundreds of millions of people worldwide that own shares and follow markets, there a probably only a few thousand that are competent and skilled at technical analysis. That is, a few thousand on earth.

It is such a difficult, time consuming skill to master, which once mastered will take hours each and every day to pour over charts and graphs that the individual must let it dominate his or her life. Mathematics and number analysis will become key components of daily life.

For the rest of us, life is just too short to spend it looking at 100 graphs and indicators each day. I know for sure that my time here is too limited for that.

So what I am saying is that it is very, very difficult to manage money successfully over the medium to long term. Heck, even a chimp throwing darts at a page of the Financial Times or Wall Street Journal will have some success, but will that success last long?

I have worked with quite a number of financial or investment advisers over the years. I would guess at over 100 by now. That may not sound like a huge number, but each one probably had between 80 and 150 regular clients. Between them then, these advisers were helping maybe 15,000 families to plan their finances.

Advising in the region of 15,000 families about money is a pretty serious responsibility. In truth, helping just one family is quite a responsibility. Trust me on that.

The vast majority of these advisers specialized in mortgages and the financial aspects of house buying. That is very understandable since most housing markets have a reliable turnover of property and therefore, a reliable source of business and income for the adviser.

Yet, all those advisers needed to be able to sit and pass annual exams relating to investments and on the odd occasion provide advice on the subject. I don't think that I am being harsh in saying that only 2 of the advisers could give investment advice competently.

In short, if you want good quality, competent investment advice, you need to do one of two things. Either be lucky and have an adviser that really is skilled in the subject or get out your chequebook and pay for quality.

Please don't misunderstand me. I'm not trying to be mean about these fellow professionals. I am simply trying to make one very direct point: there is so much investment information out there that one person can never 'know it all'. In fact, it's really close to impossible to know a lot.

Firstly, I believe, we should start with a realization.

The stock exchange is rarely a place where anyone 'gets rich quick'. Offhand, I don't know where anyone does that, but certainly not in investments. Sure, some occasional stocks and shares will rise quickly making their owners money, but rarely will you become rich. Bear in mind that if an investment doubles in one year (which is pretty rare) you needed to be already wealthy to make a lot of money. If you invested a thousand, you will have just 'made' a thousand. You aren't wealthy or rich yet.

Second realization is this ... It isn't easy. If everyone could become a billionaire by investing, Warren Buffett would not be famous. It takes time, study and effort and most importantly - independent thought. Not everyone has the will or stamina to carry that through. I know that mine wavers from time to time. Who doesn't suffer setbacks and confidence knocks?

Thirdly, though it may be a 'hobby', it isn't 'fun'. The world of investment is dominated by investment banks and their bankers. They do all the big deals, float companies, issue bonds, trade stocks, bonds, currencies and commodities and make lots of money. They employ some of the world's brightest young MBA's to figure out new and improved profit making ventures. They do all this because it is a business, with real money and real profits. Nobody is playing around.

If you want to be successful, you too need to view it as a business. Here is tip number one: if you are interested, go and do some reading about Benjamin Graham. Buy his books and digest. It will take a while, but it is the proper place to start. It was Ben Graham that first coined the idea successful investment is businesslike.

All that said, the little guy can still make money investing. I know, I do. I'm not rich and I don't make a fortune, but it all helps. Why can't you do something similar? Big funds find it hard to invest in small companies, maybe that offers you an edge. Often, money managers are so busy working their 15 hour days that they miss wider discoveries in society. Just by going to the mall or supermarket, you might spot lines selling well and get a head start on the analysts. If that approach sounds good, you might like to grab a book by Peter Lynch - he offers guidance on how he finds winners, or as he puts it 'ten baggers'.

If you really want to do well in investment on the stock exchange, then you need to approach it as if it were your own business. A part-time business perhaps, but still a business. That also means taking your information sources seriously. There are many portfolio tracking systems online, some free and others require monthly payment - get registered to one! There are magazines that follow and report on stock markets and shares each week - subscribe to one!

If initially, you just start reading and trying to understand what the heck those guys are on about ... you will make progress. It is better than investing blindly.

A stock exchange, for beginners can be a daunting way to make a second income. Fear not, with time, you can learn the skills. But, I warn you again that it takes effort, independent thought and study to really do well.

Best Stock Formations for Beginners

One of the most important aspects of learning to read stock charts and using Technical Analysis is to remember that the Market Structure is changing and evolving over time. Sometimes these changes are very slow, other times the evolution is occurring at a rapid pace. In the past 5 years, the pace of change has been accelerating and continues to move at an ever increasing level. Therefore, new and novice investors and traders need to be aware that all of the older books, articles, and information on the internet and in bookstores must be studied but also accepted as being outdated.

The topping formations that are developing now in the market reflect the fact that now 70-80% of all the market orders are automated. What this means is that most of the orders are triggered by a computer. Market Makers used to be humans that made the market by filling orders when there was no counter order. Now most of the market maker orders are fully automated.

Computer generated and matched orders create different technical patterns including topping formations, than human initiated and typed in orders. In addition, the increased use of Alternative Trading Systems platforms by the giant institutions aka ATS, High Frequency Trading Firms Algorithmic trading HFTs, Electronic Communication Networks ECNs, and 16 different US stock Exchanges, create a far more dynamic stock market than what was present just a few years ago.

To start understanding topping action, a new or novice investor or trader must learn the original classic topping formations. Then they must learn the new topping formations of the automated marketplace. When both are learned, the investor or trader is prepared to use stock charts and technical analysis to the fullest advantage and success.

The Original Topping Formations and Patterns:

A topping formation occurs when a stock has been moving up for a long period of time and speculation has entered the price action. Often stock prices will go vertical with huge gains or shrinking price action just before a topping pattern begins. Tops often take a long time to form because most traders and investors don't want to believe the uptrend is over. Late comers frequently buy a stock that is topping when it "dips" in price, because they are unaware of the fact that the stock has reached the end of its long term or intermediate term uptrend, needs to correct and move down.

This late buying causes tops to form over an extended period of time with a variety of topping patterns. Sometimes a top comes swiftly and the price collapses, but usually it takes a while. Regardless of your trading or investing style, being able to recognize topping formations early will help you keep more of your profits by exiting before the stock falls.

The Four Original Classic Textbook Topping Formations are:

1. Inverted V is the opposite of a bottoming stock V. The inverted V occurs when a stock has been running up so fast that it doesn't develop any viable support levels, suddenly peaks and forms a sheer cliff drop on the other side. These often have gap downs and the runs are so fast downward that they can be tough to catch. Inverted V tops are rarer now due to how High Frequency Trader activity controls most topping formations.

2. The Double Top is an inverted W or what is usually called an "M Top." This is

where the stock reaches a high, retraces and then moves up again but is unable to move beyond the original previous high to continue up. It then proceeds to move down again. The confirmation that a reversal of trend has occurred is when the price of the stock violates the lows of the M formation. Double tops are not topping formations until the reversal is signaled. Double tops can easily turn into a longer term sideways pattern that meanders up and down within that price range, so confirmation of price is critical. Also Double or M Tops are less common and rarely form on long term trends. With the automated market, most M Tops are seen only on the short term trend.

3. Triple Tops and Head & Shoulders are basically that the H&S formation is a variation of the Triple Top. Head & Shoulders Topping Formations are exceedingly rare nowadays. Triple Tops are also quite rare. The rule for H&S is that it must break the neckline, which is the lows between the shoulders. The neckline

can be horizontal or angled and either makes no significant difference in the success of the downside formation. The head should be formed on upside weaker volume, the right shoulder should form on upside weaker volume still, and the break to the downside should form with strong red or downside volume.

These tops are very rare nowadays due to how the giant funds use ATS platforms to slowly sell out of a stock long before it runs up speculatively. The H&S formation peak fails to form often as HFTs trigger massive collapsing sell-offs on sudden news events. Since HFTs are mostly one day events the "Head" that used to form, no longer forms because there is no continuation after the huge one-day volume surge and price speculative intraday action.

4. The Rounding Top is the opposite of the rounding bottom and is very ominous and reliable. Rounding tops usually form slowly giving the holder time to exit. They can be short term or long term formations. The

Rounding Top used to be less common but now is forming on all 3 trends, long term aka primary, intermediate term, and even the short term trend. The Rounding Top is harder to identify early on but is a pattern all investors and traders need to learn and identify as early as possible to protect more profits. The Rounding Top can fall quickly, and has less support on the way down to prior lows.

Topping formations on the 3 Trend timeframes of Long Term, Intermediate Term, and Short Term are caused by different fundamental situations. The Long Term Trend top starts when the company has reached market pre-saturation of its main products or services. The overall stock market topping occurs either when several major new technology industries have reached market saturation, or speculation has entered a Bull Market causing extreme angles of ascent on the long term trend for most stocks, or due to a relational impact of a different Financial Market that is collapsing.

For the Intermediate Term Trend, a topping action is usually related more to industries and sectors, and most stocks in that industry or sector will peak at similar intervals. The Short Term Trend is mostly individual companies that have a weaker quarter, or have cyclical earnings and revenues, or where an unexpected event has hampered the growth of the company. Regardless of all of the technical patterns you can learn, all tops are based on fundamental issues, financial market interrelationships, or a sudden unexpected Black Swan event such as a banking debacle.

Tops are caused by short term trading action. Market tops as opposed to individual stock tops, can take quite a bit of time to form. Individual stocks can often top rather rapidly. Contrarian indicators will show extreme readings prior to market tops for 2-4 months or longer before the market top actually occurs. This is because of the buying that takes place as a top forms. Individual stocks will show nearly vertical trend lines if the buying that caused the top has become irrational and without solid basis, and is therefore pure gambling and get rich speculation.

Contrarian views are tough for beginners. It is really hard to jump onto the other side of the bank of the fast flowing river of trading and emotion. No one likes to be the lone man out. That is why most highly successful traders are loners and do not participate in group chat rooms. You have to be able to make a call or decision and stick with it even when others think you are wrong. Contrarian also only works when the market goes to an extreme. It doesn't work when the market is slightly overbought or slightly oversold. It has to be an extreme.

During a topping formation it is likely that the stock price will go from one extreme high to another, and then another again before it collapses. Rarely is that first extreme the end of the price high. The reason is the odd-lot buyer and the small uninformed buyer who has very little knowledge about the market. Their market orders can drive prices much higher. Then there are the High Frequency Trading Companies HFTs using computer generated algorithms that trigger thousands of orders on the millisecond scale, that create the daily feeding frenzy second by second. HFTs can and do cause major price fluctuations during the trading day.

Individual Day Traders are only permitted to trade on the minute timeframe and those orders are filled on a mandatory 90 seconds. HFTs trade 1000-3000 times per second. That means individual Day Trader minute order can't see the 60,000 to 90,000 HFT orders that are being processed and changing price during that one minute the Day Trader order is being filled. Therefore, individual Day Traders are constantly at a disadvantage in terms of seeing what HFT orders are doing to price on the millisecond scale. That is why the SEC has sent out messages warning individual traders of the hazards and huge risk of Day Trading in the automated marketplace.

For beginners trying to trade a market in an extreme mode can be very dangerous and tricky as the volatility increases with each level of price speculation. It is a wave of euphoric buying that is totally without any logic or rational. My advice for most beginners is not to trade live but to paper trade and learn. Once you have a 75-80% success rate on a professional style simulator, not the "game simulators" promoted to the general crowd, then you will be ready to trade the stock market.

I also advise avoiding Day Trading if you are an individual trader, because this has become an extremely risky style in the past few years. Instead consider Swing trading, Position trading, or Intermediate term trading all of which provide far superior profits

# Chapter 10: Major Stock Exchanges

The stock market has a few major stock exchanges that are worth talking about in more detail. These markets are where most of the volume and liquidity (money) will be, thus the markets that have the most movement and profit to offer.

The Four Major Exchanges

## NYSE

The New York Stock Exchange sees about $13.4 trillion in movement a day. The NYSE is the largest stock exchange in the world in terms of trade volume. It is also located in a physical location like all stock exchanges. The NYSE regulates stocks, commodities, and other product exchanges. Companies from around the world list their IPOs on the NYSE to gain the attention of investors. Companies can be locally listed on their country's exchange and then launch on the NYSE when they become large enough to sustain the interest in their shares.

Companies can only be listed on one exchange at a time to avoid regulatory issues and some countries do not allow their companies to list on the NYSE. Any stock listed on the NYSE can be purchased by traders to make a profit and earn dividends.

In North America, there is more than one exchange like the Philadelphia exchange and Toronto. However, it is the NYSE, Dow index, and NASDAQ that get the most media. The Dow Jones and NASDAQ will not be discussed in this section because they relate more to stock performance and options exchanges.

Tokyo Stock Exchange

Japan's stock exchange is the TSE and it sees $3.8 trillion in movement per day, although in 2014 it was listed as $4 trillion. The Tosho (TSE) is considered the third largest in terms of market cap, but the number of companies listed are only 2,292 making it the fourth largest for the amount of companies listed on the exchange. In 2012, the TSE merged with Osaka Securities Exchange to become the JPX or Japan Exchange Group. The exchange runs from 9am to 11:30 am and from 12:30 to 3pm during the weekdays. These are hours based on the Asian time zone.

**LSE**

The London Stock Exchange dealt with approximately $3.6 trillion market movement for the day prior to 2014. The LSE was formed in 1801 and as of 2014 had $6.06 trillion as a market cap. The London Stock Exchange is considered the second largest by market cap data; however, it is behind the NASDAQ in terms of overall size. The LSE has merged with certain exchanges like Borsa Italiana, MTS, Turquoise, NASDAQ Bids, and there is a proposed merger with TMX Group. The LSE has primary markets with premium listed main market companies, which are the biggest UK markets. There is the Alternative Investment Market for smaller companies, professional securities market, and a specialist fund market. The LSE is open daily, on weekdays from 8am to 4:30pm, GMT.

**Euronext**

This is the European Stock Exchange. It was smaller dealing with only $2.9 trillion in market movement per day prior to the split with the NYSE. In 2015, the exchange started seeing closer to $3.7 trillion as a market cap. This was after Euronext made a public offering to become a separate entity. The market offers equities, exchange traded funds, bonds, derivatives, commodities, warrants and certificates, and indices. It was established as an exchange in Amsterdam, London, Brussels, Paris, and Lisbon, as well as part of the Intercontinental Exchange.

Other Popular and Major Exchanges

In this list you will see three other major exchanges, which are popular in certain markets like Asian stock investments. They are listed because they have a higher market cap in comparison to other exchanges that exist around the world.

Shanghai Stock Exchange

Shanghai is another Asian market that sees a fairly high volume at $2.7 trillion.

Hong Kong Stock Exchange

Hong Kong has the same amount of traffic as the Shanghai Market.

Toronto Stock Exchange

Toronto is home to Canada's stock exchange. The market cap for this exchange is $2.2 trillion.

Stock Market Performance and Indexes

The NASDAQ and Dow Jones are two important indexes to discuss, and determine market performance. Each needs to be discussed in their own right to help you understand how the stock market works.

**NASDAQ**

The NASDAQ is a stock exchange that also offers options trading. NASDAQ stands for National Association of Securities Dealers Automated Quotations. It was started in 1971 as the National Association of Securities Dealers. It is an exchange that was the first electronic stock market, which lowered the spread charged to investors. The spread is the difference between the buy and sell price, and is where most brokerage firms make their money. The NASDAQ offers a premarket period to fit into the London Stock Exchange, which is a part of the trading system. These hours are 4am to 9:30am EST and then from 9:30am to 4pm for the normal trading session. There is also a post market session that fits in the Asian time zone trading period and those hours are 4pm to 8pm.

The NASDAQ has market tiers: small, mid, and large cap. They are referred to as the capital, global, and global select market, respectively.

The stock exchange sees $9.6 trillion in daily movement. Approximately 3,600 companies are listed on the exchange. Investors can do more on the NASDAQ with options trading than on other exchanges. Options are a complicated process that you will want advanced stock market investing information to understand. For now, you just need to know it is an exchange with a different list of companies than the NYSE that may offer you room to grow into options trading.

The Dow Jones

The Dow Jones Industrial Average is a stock market index. A stock market index will measure the value of a specific section of the stock market. It is computed based on selected stocks based on an average of the price of these shares. Investors use it to figure out the market movement and market health based on the average prices of top companies. Mutual funds and exchange traded funds tend to use this type of index to track what the funds will do or have done in reacting to news and economic data. The Dow Jones was the first stock market index to be started. It was devised by Charles Dow in 1896. Edward Jones, was his partner and a statistician. They weight 30 components that have to do with traditional industries.

Stock market investors will use the Dow Jones to determine the performance of a specific industry sector for American companies and overall weighting of the USAs economic stability. The Dow Jones is not meant to be influenced by economic reports or corporate reports, but by price movement alone.

You can use the Dow Jones for ETF, leverage, short funds, future contracts and options contracts.

When you hear media experts talking about the market going up or down by a certain number of "points," they are usually talking about the Dow Jones index computation.

# Chapter 11: How To Purchase Stocks

Earlier, we took some time to explore the things that you should look at to find the perfect stocks to invest in. You want to make sure that you pick out stocks that will actually bring you money, ones that have good management, steady profits, and manageable debts so that you can make money. After you have done some research on the stock market, it is time to enter the market and actually purchase the stocks that you want to invest in. Let's take a look at how you enter the market by purchasing stocks.

Use a broker

Since you are a beginner and you have not had the opportunity to work in the stock market yet, it may be a good idea to work with a broker. The broker will help you make smart decisions when it comes to the stocks that you should invest in. Brokers spend their time learning how to work with the market, and they have been doing work in this industry for many years. They have a lot of experience and expertise that is needed to help you make good decisions. Beginners can really benefit from taking the advice from a broker they trust.

There are actually a few types of brokers that you can choose to work with and it will depend on how much you would like to spend on the broker and how much advice you will end up needing. The first broker that you can work with is a full-service broker. This type of broker will be responsible for managing all of the stocks and purchases that happen on your account. You will be able to consult with them about any purchases that you are considering and the best steps that you can take to grow your portfolio. You can give some instructions and provide your opinion, but they will take over most of the work for your investment for you. If you have no idea what you are doing and you would like someone to hold your hand, the full-service broker is a good option for you.

Another option for brokers is to work with what is known as a discount broker. These brokers will cost you less than a full-service broker, but remember that it also means you will receive fewer services from them. You must put in more time and effort to get your investments done. However, they will help you to save some money and can really assist you to get some of the advice that you need in the investment world.

Consider a reinvestment plan

You can, while you are working on which stocks to go with, decide to work with one individual company. When you work with this company, you can take the profits that you earn through dividends, and then use that money to purchase more stocks through the same company. As you are first getting started, you will find that you may not be able to invest much, which will limit how many stocks you are able to purchase. When you take that money and reinvest it to get more stocks, rather than taking and personally using the money for your own reasons, can help you to get more profit in the future because you will own more stocks. Over time, your money will start to grow more, and it can help to reduce your risk of investing all at the same time.

Direct investing plans

Since you are a new investor, you will be able to choose whether you would like to work with a direct investment plan. With this kind of investment, you would not have to use a broker to make your purchases, which will save you some fees that you would spend on that person. For this one, you will choose to work directly with the individual company that you want to invest in. You will not go through the stock exchange, but rather, you will go through the company directly to purchase your stocks. There will be a few extra fees that will come with using this option, but they are smaller than what you will find with a broker, so it is a good way to save some money.

This one can be considered similar to the last option, but you will still be able to keep the dividends when you are done, rather than reinvesting those profits. You could choose to use that money to purchase more stocks, but it is not necessary to be considered a direct investment plan. You may want to work with this option if you feel like working with only one company and you don't think that working with a broker is necessary.

All of these options will help you to get your foot in the door of the stock market so that you can start to invest and earn a profit. Remember that in the beginning, you will probably only make a little bit of money, and you may even need to bring in a broker to do the work for you if you are confused, but the point is that you get started and find the option that works the best for you. Take a look through some of the options above and find the one that is sure to fit your style and give you the profits that you want.

# Chapter 12: Researching Your Stocks

You can't go to war without a weapon. You can't just buy a stock, you must do extensive research. You must learn to be your own stock analyst. This will help you make a wise and sound investment decision.

To do a comprehensive stock research, you must use two methods used in Economics – micro-economics analysis and macro-economic analysis.

Macro-Economic Analysis

Economic forces such as the law of supply and demand affect stock prices. So, before you invest in a stock, you have to use a top-down global research approach. You must look at the global trends. You must look at the big picture

As of writing Airbnb is not a public company yet. But, for the purpose of discussion, let's assume that it is. A lot of cities in Europe and in the United States have banned Airbnb. But, it continues to grow in various cities in the world. In fact, you can find a lot of great Airbnb deals in Bali, Malaysia, Singapore, Zurich, Mykonos, and Faro. Plus, it still has a number of untapped markets. If you look at the big picture, you'll see that Airbnb is still a great investment because of its huge growth potential.

Aside from looking at the company's global overview, you must also consider other factors, such as:

Interest Rates

When the interest rate is high, it would be more costly for companies and individual to pay their debts. This decreases their disposable income and their spending. This affects business revenues and can drive down the stock prices.

But, when a country has a low interest rate, people have more disposable income. They'll end up buying more stuff. This could lead to an increase in stock prices.

But, you have to take note that rising interest rates can benefit specific industries, such as the financial sector – banks, mortgage companies, lending companies, and insurance companies.

Cyclical nature of an industry

Before you buy a company's stock, you have to determine if that company belongs to a cyclical industry.

Cyclical sectors such as the automobile industry and the construction industry are sensitive to the ups and downs of the economy. When the economy is good, their prices go up, but it goes down when there's a recession.

Try to avoid investing in companies in cyclical sectors (unless you're very good at timing your investments). You'd want to invest in a stock that can stand economic setbacks.

You must examine the stock market index.

An index tracks the performance of market leaders. So, it pretty much reflects the overall health of the stock market. If an index is trending up, it means that stock market players are a bit optimistic and a Bull Market may be happening.

Industry-wide research.

Let's say that you want to invest in luxury brands such as Louis Vuitton (LVMH) or YSL. Before you do that, you must look into the overall health of that industry.

If you look closely, you might discover that luxury brands are not doing as well as they used to be because of online shops and China-made products.

Micro- Economic Analysis

When you do macro-economic analysis, you are looking at the economy and the industry. But, micro-economic analysis uses a "bottom-up" approach. This means that you have to do extensive company research.

You have to look into the different aspects of the company, such as:

a)The company's product – Is the product good? Does it have loyal customers? Is the product going to be relevant ten years from now? Let's say that a music store is selling its stocks. Would you buy it? Well, let's face it, no one buys CDs anymore. We just download music from the internet or check YouTube. Technology is changing by the minute. A widely used product may become irrelevant and unnecessary in the next few years. Just look at what happened to diskettes.

b)Sales and revenue – Is the company earning money? Are their products doing well in the market?

c) Debt to Equity ratio – Is the company's debt bigger than its equity? If so, then you should run as fast as you can.

d)P/E ratio – If the company has a high P/E ratio, it means that it has a high growth potential. But, it also means that the stock is overvalued. A low P/E ratio means that the company has low growth potential, but it also means that it's overvalued. If you're into growth investing, choose a company with high P/E. But, you have to choose a company with low P/E if you're into value investing.

e)Earnings per share or EPS – A company with high EPS is really doing well. It's profitable. So, assuming other factors check out (e.g. if it's not using a lot of unsustainable debt to generate the earnings), it's a good idea to invest in a company with a high EPS.

f) Company management – Do you trust the people managing the company? Do they engage in unethical business practices? If you don't trust the people running the company, then avoid it at all cost.

Also, make sure that the company's profit is trending upward at least in the last five years

# Chapter 13: The Must-Know Stock Market Terms

If you are to be successful at stock market investing, it is important that you know some stock market terms that you are likely to come across.

Stock Split

In most cases, publicly traded companies have a particular number of outstanding shares on the stock market. A stock split is a decision by the board of directors to increase the number of shares outstanding by issuing shares to current shareholders. For instance, in a 2 for 1 stock split, each shareholder who has one share is given an additional share. Therefore, if you had 10,000 shares, you end up having 20,000 shares. In a stock split, the price of the share is also affected. After the split in the above case, the stock price will be halved. Therefore, even though the number of outstanding shares has increased, and the stock price has changed, market capitalization remains constant.

Companies usually do a stock split when they see their share price increase too high or beyond the price levels of similar firms in the sector. Basically, the goal is to make the shares look more affordable to small investors even if the underlying company value has not changed.

**Dividends**

When you buy shares to become one of the company's shareholders, the company can pay you a part of their profits, known as dividends. However, the company's directors might decide not to pay out dividends, but rather use the money earned for growth and expansion.

If you want to get a good income, you can invest in a company that is known to pay their shareholders high dividends even if the share price does not increase as much in value. You can then use your dividends to buy more shares for even higher returns if the value of the shares goes up.

According to the Barclays Equity Gilt Study, which was carried out to find out the results of investing long-term, if you invest over a period of ten years, your average return on investment annually from inflation-adjusted stock is 5%. If you reinvest your dividends, you get the benefit of compounding interest.

The study utilized data that dates back to the 19th century to show the significance of reinvesting your dividend income. If 100 pounds were invested in equities in the late 1800s, it would be 191 pounds now if no reinvestments were made. However, if the dividends were reinvested, the amount would accrue to 28,386 pounds.

Ask or Offer

This refers to the lowest price that someone is willing to sell the security for.

Bear Market

This is a kind of market where the stock prices keep falling.

**Beta**

This is simply a measurement that shows the relationship between the stock price and the movement of the market.

**Bid**

This is the highest price at which a buyer is willing to pay for a security.

Bull Market

This is a market where stock prices keep rising.

**Ex-Dividend**

If you purchase ex-dividend shares, you are not entitled to the upcoming dividend that has already been declared.

On-Stop Order

This is a term that is used to refer to the intention of trading at a later time when the stock price reaches a particular top price.

Penny Stocks

These are low-priced stocks that sell at less than $1.00 a share

## Bonus Issue

This is when a company issues you dividends in the form of shares instead of cash.

## Rights Issue

This is when current shareholders can purchase shares at a special price based on their holdings of old shares. The share price in a right issue is usually lower than the market price.

## Blue-Chip Stocks

Although blue-chip stocks have a reputation for being stodgy, boring and even outdated, they have worked wonders for the lives of non-profit foundations, retirees, and even conservative people because they can generate so much money over a long period of time. The phrase 'blue-chip' comes from the game poker where the most valuable chips are the color blue. The kind of companies that offer blue-chip stocks are usually top companies in America with a rich history.

Blue-chips are all about making profits; hence, their prosaic nature is not deserved. If you invest in blue-chip stocks, you can hold them for many decades, and it usually means that your family has access to a lifetime stream of income through dividends.

A relatively subjective criterion is used to categorize a company's shares as blue-chip. According to many professionals, blue-chip stocks have various attributes that are similar, including:

❖ High commercial paper and bond market credit ratings.

❖ Strong balance sheets with an average burden of debt.

❖ A competitive market place advantage due to franchise value, cost efficiency, or even control of distribution.

❖ A record of many decades of established stable earning potential.

❖ A large size of market capitalization and revenue in relation to businesses in America.

❖ Diversified geographic location as in the case of Coca-Cola, and varied product lines as in the case of General Electric.

❖ Long dividend payment records to holders of common stock that are uninterrupted.

❖ The dividends you receive increase in value payable to each shareholder.

The Industrial Average of Dow Jones

The majority of blue-chip companies make use of the industrial average, Dow Jones, to ensure that their positions in the industry remain the same. With great credit ratings and average levels of debt these companies can borrow money at a lower cost than their counterparts (their competitors) in the marketplace. Customers like you are more likely to buy a product from a brand with an excellent reputation in the market, despite being more expensive.

The Dow Jones Industrial Average is the most popular blue-chip company list. 'The Wall Street Journal' editors choose a list of 30 stocks, and for a company to appear in this list, it must be an industry leader. In order for the Dow Jones to come up with a comprehensive list of prestigious blue-chip companies, potential companies are thoroughly scrutinized. Due to blue-chip stocks' inherent stability, the companies making up the Dow Jones index almost never changes.

Blue-Chip Stock Investment

You can invest in blue-chip stock in a number of ways. You can buy stock directly via a direct stock buying plan, a broker, or even a dividend reinvestment plan. You can also buy a blue-chip stock mutual fund, or ETF (Exchange Traded Fund), like the Industrial Average of SPDR Dow Jones that is known to feature a portfolio that reflects the index it is named after. By investing in this kind of stock, you get shares in big companies like McDonald's, Exxon Mobil, Walmart, Microsoft, Coca-Cola, and Disney, among others, for a low expense-ratio and one brokerage commission.

Although you can sell your blue-chip stock, it is always a difficult decision that must be thought over seriously.

Stock Market Capitalization

This simply refers to the market value of the outstanding shares of a company. For example, if Coca-Cola Company has 2 million shares, each at $50, the company's market capitalization would be $100 million. Market capitalization can help you compare and understand the size of two different companies.

Disadvantages of Market Capitalization

Market capitalization has some shortcomings that you should know as someone planning to venture into this market. For one, it cannot be used when looking into the debt of a company. When you buy stock in a company, its true worth is its market capitalization minus its debts, and that is what is known as an enterprise value.

Portfolio Development Using Market Capitalization

When you become a professional investor in this market, like many others, you get to divide your portfolio by the size of the company's market capitalization. This technique can enable you to exploit the stability of larger companies with greater stability and high dividend payouts, and smaller companies with faster historical growth. When you start investing in the stock market, you will come across the following categories of market capitalization: micro, small, mid, large and mega-caps.

Microcap is a company whose market capitalization is below $300 million, small cap $300 million to $2 billion, mid-cap $2 billion to $10 billion, large-cap $10 billion to $50 billion, and mega-cap over $50 billion.

# Chapter 14: Picking The Right Stock

As I mentioned before, there are tons and tons of different variables that determine if a stock will increase in value, decrease in value, or stay the same. Stocks can follow trends and show patterns as their values increase or decrease, or they may suddenly change with very little or no warning. So, with all of these different variables, how do you pick the stock that has the potential to make you money? There are a few different strategies that can help you decide on a stock:

Know the Basic Information Regarding the Company

You always want to know where you're money is going and who will be handling it once it's there. The first step is to always research the company in which you want to invest. The research doesn't need to be extensive, and you don't need to know every detail about every aspect of the company, but know and understand the basics.

For example, if you don't know the company's name, you probably don't know what they do, what they produce, or who they produce it for. Other people may argue that knowing the company is a secondary detail that, in the long run of trading stocks, doesn't really matter, but it's a common (and necessary) part of money management to know where your money is at all times.

For any and all companies from which you buy stocks, know what they do. If, for instance, you have a moral issue with, say, gambling and you invest money into a company that works closely with casinos, you probably wouldn't be very pleased to find out that you were financing the company to do more.

Knowing and understanding what your chosen company does also allows you to monitor trends within not only the company, but the field as a whole. Confused? Read the next section to fully grasp what I mean.

Look for Trends with the Stock

Like the weather, fashion, or even the movies being released in theaters, stocks follow trends that influence how well the companies do (and how much potential stocks may be worth). Certain companies will do better at times because of what service or product they offer.

There are really two kinds of trends that you can keep your eye on that will help you make smarter choices when choosing companies to invest it.

The first type of trend is simply the trend of the stock. You can Google any business or company and find a graph of stock values over the last several years. Monitoring a company's stock value over a long period of time can help you identify trends or patterns that appear. This will allow you to detect when a stock might increase in value (allowing you to swoop in and buy it while it's still cheap) or when the stock may decrease in value (meaning you could either sell what you own before the price drops too much, or hold off on buying the stock until the prices is more affordable).

Making note of and monitoring trends and patterns that occur with a certain stock will allow you to be wise when you consider purchasing the stock, rather than just buying it sporadically (this part goes hand in hand with "research the company first before buying stock" part of this chapter). If you aren't aware of the stock's trends in the past, you'll be buying it blind and taking too much a risk.

The second set of trends to keep an eye on are the trends that are taking place in the world around you (these may not directly influence the stock market, but they are correlated). Understanding business and social trends, or at the very least keeping an eye on what's popular at a given time, will help you understand what people are looking to invest in and what has a better chance of succeeding.

Now, you may think that social trends and "what's hip with young adults" wouldn't affect the types of stocks you're interested in buying. That is where you are so very wrong.

Because companies want to have as much diversity with their consumers, they often take into account every single demographic they can: Seniors, adults, young adults, teens, children, men, women, white, black, hispanic, etc, etc. The list can go one forever. Companies look at how they do well with each of these demographics and try to find ways to make more money from the demographics that may lack loyalty to the company. How do they do this? They research. They ask themselves "what are kids into these days?" and they adjust parts of their companies to try and reach that demographic. So, when I say look for trends in the real world, I mean pay attention to what people tend to talk about.

Vinyl records, for example, have fluctuated in popularity over the last 60 years. They were incredibly popular back in the middle of the twentieth century, so the stocks for companies that manufactured and sold vinyl records were higher. Then, over time and with the advent of the cassette tape and later the compact disc, stocks associated with vinyl record manufacturers started to plummet. Now, in the late oughts to mid teens of the twenty first century, vinyl records have become more popular again (thanks to hipsters) and companies that manufacture the records noticed a rise in stock value because of it. Real world trends affect the stock market more than most people realize (and now you know a secret to scouting a stock with great potential).

Diversify, Diversify, Diversify All of Your Investments!

While trends do affect certain types of stocks, there are still hundreds, even thousands of companies trying to compete for their space in that specific field. Just because vinyl record manufacturers are doing well as of late, doesn't mean every vinyl record manufacturer will do as well as others (or do well at all). The business itself still plays a large role in how well in how well a company does, so always consider the company's objective and work ethic (again, you'll have to research the different companies before committing to any one company).

Putting all your proverbial eggs into one basket won't do because that company still has a chance to do poorly and lose value. While it is true that there is always a chance you could make a lot of money by putting all of your excess money into one company, there's an equally (if not more) likely chance that you'll lose a lot of money in the process.

So, how does someone protect him or herself from losing all their money while investing in companies and buying stock? He diversifies where he invests his money.

Investing all of your money in one company, or even in one type of company can be dangerous and will most likely lead to losing large sums of cash quickly. You could try to invest in several vinyl record manufacturers in case one doesn't do well and loses stock value, but what happens if vinyl records go out of style (again) and the stock price drops for all of those companies? Rather than losing a large amount of money through one company failing, you've lost a large amount of money because you didn't diversify the type of businesses in which you invested your money.

Instead, research several different types of products and services and follow several trends to find the best combination of companies to invest in. Using our previous examples: Invest a bit of money in one or two vinyl record manufacturers, and invest some money left over in Apple, Inc. or another computer developer. That way, if one product begins to lose popularity and consumer demand (which is a large indicator of how well a stock's potential is), you'll have a second company selling a different product to make up for at least some of the loses you encounter.

Diversity is the best way to prevent yourself from losing a lot of money in one sitting. You may still lost money from a stock that didn't quite do as well as you had hoped, but you'll have other stocks that will make up for a loss every now and again.

Limit Your Options until You're Comfortable

Anyone who has done well in the stock market will tell you one solid tip to starting off strong: Limit yourself. Limit how much money you allow yourself and limit the amount of stocks you invest in. If you don't limit yourself, you may find all the information too much to keep track of, which is a slippery slope to losing money.

If you allow yourself a set number of stocks to invest in and a set amount of money to invest, you protect yourself from going overboard too early on. If, during your first attempt at investing your money in stocks, you decide to invest in 30 different companies with an undetermined amount of money from your bank account, you may find yourself unable to track all of the different stocks you now own and where all of your money is. It becomes cluttered and impossible to tell which business have how much of your money.

To start, set a limit that's easy to note and keep track of. Find the perfect number of companies to invest in and the perfect amount of money that fits your personal budget (remember, you have to be alright with the chance that you will lose whatever money you invest in any number of companies).

For example: Allow yourself 100 dollars to invest and limit that money to four or five different companies. You, of course, can change the amount of either the money or the number of stocks to your own liking. Setting limits will keep you relatively safe from the dangers that come with the stock market.

What's more important is to never, ever go past your limit. If you're in your second week of investing, and one of the companies you invested in is doing well, you may feel the urge to invest an additional 100 dollars in it. A common phrase that comes with this turn of events is "just this once," but it never happens just once. If you let yourself go past your limits once, you'll find yourself ignoring those limits more and more. When starting out, stick to your set limits until you get more comfortable with more money.

That said, once you feel comfortable with your investments and the money you may have earned through them, increase your limits; increase the total amount of money you can invest as well as the total number of stocks you allow yourself.

Be Passionate about the Company Succeeding

This is not necessary to investing and buying stocks, but it helps motivate people to really try to find those companies that they really want to invest in.

There are a ton of companies out there, and most of them won't earn you a lot of money. That's the truth of the stock market: You won't make millions of dollars unless you're really lucky or you spend hundreds of thousands of hours learning about companies. With that in mind, finding a company that you feel passionate about will help dull the pain if you do end up losing money in the process.

What do I mean by being "passionate" about a company? Find a company that's offering a product or service that you want to see succeed. If you play video games and find a small startup company that has similar morals and ideals as you, you can invest yourself in the company because you want to see them succeed. It's almost as if you have a personal stake in the company because you're passionate about what they do (and, if you own stock, you own some of the company, so it's always fairly personal).

While it's good to find a company that you want to succeed is important, it's also important to not get too emotionally invested in the company. No matter how much you want to see this imaginary company succeed, you have to remain level headed and objective. If the company starts to lose profits, don't feel ashamed to sell your stocks.

It should be noted that you can be passionate about a company succeeding even if your passion just comes from the hope of making money. Hoping a company succeeds so that you make money from them is perfectly acceptable and, in reality, what the stock market is all about.

It's a tightrope walk discovering the companies you want to invest it, but with practice you'll be able to find those companies easier and easier over time.

Find Companies that Offer a "Safer" Investment Opportunity

Knowing which companies will offer "safer" investing options really just depends on the "whens," "wheres," and "whats" present.

The "when" refers to the time of buying. Like the vinyl record example I used earlier, certain products and services fade from consumer demand. Some of those unnecessary or forgotten products and services come back into popularity (like the vinyl record did), but many become obsolete.

The "where" refer to the company's location in the world. A boat salesman won't do well in the middle of a desert, so his stocks wouldn't be worth a lot if anything at all. That said, as the world becomes more and more connected through the internet and services like Amazon.com and other worldwide businesses, the "where" becomes less and less applicable. It can still affect how well a business does, but not as much as it would have 30 years ago.

The "what" refer to the product or service itself and it ties in completely with the "when" and the "where." What does the company offer and is it demanded in the world today? Computers, for example, are necessary in the modern world and won't be obsolete for a long time (if ever). Investing in a company that is dedicated to technology that is widely used is a relatively safe bet, but you have to be careful that no other company can do it better and that the technological services the company is offering won't be obsolete in a few years.

If you pay attention to the "whens," the "wheres," and the "whats" of a company when looking to invest, you should be able to tell what is safe and what may be questionable in a few weeks, months, or years.

Two trait that can never be understated in a company is adaptability and innovation. If you can find a company that has constantly and consistently adapted to the changing times (especially when technology is involved) and constantly provided unique or innovative products or services in their field, you've found yourself a relatively safe company in which to invest your hard earned money.

Know How Many Stocks to Buy and From How Many Different Companies

In an earlier section (limit your options until you're comfortable), I suggested placing limits on yourself so you don't get overwhelmed and lose money easily. This is still true. Don't dive in too quickly (you have all the time in the world to learn). Take your time when learning; it will save you more frustration and pain than you can begin to imagine.

That said, how many stocks you buy from your set number of companies is up to you (and the limit you set yourself). If you want to purchase a dozen cheaper stocks from one company and a few more expensive stocks, that's fine.

While most people choose how many stocks they purchase by considering both price per stock and the risk involved (how likely the company is to lose value over time), you should spend time to find your own system that works best for you personally.

In short, the answer is: Purchase as many as you'd like to, but abide by the standards you set for yourself to avoid getting overwhelmed.

# Conclusion

If you want to learn how you could make money efficiently and make huge profits by investing only small amounts of money, we have shown you that you should choose to invest in the stock market. There are only some people who know how to invest in the stock market because they have learned how to do so. If you follow the information in this book, you can learn how to do this too. You will gather plenty of information about stocks and the different types of stocks you can invest in. This book also sheds some light on the different techniques you can use to invest                in                stocks. As a beginner, you may make mistakes when you start investing in stocks. This is absolutely fine because you will start off with a small amount of money. But you cannot do this in the future because you will tend to invest larger amounts of money. It is important that you always learn from the mistakes that you make. Remember, every experienced trader also made mistakes at the start, but they always learned from their mistakes. It is this experience that will help you do well in the market. I hope the information in this book helps you excel at trading in the stock market.

# About the author

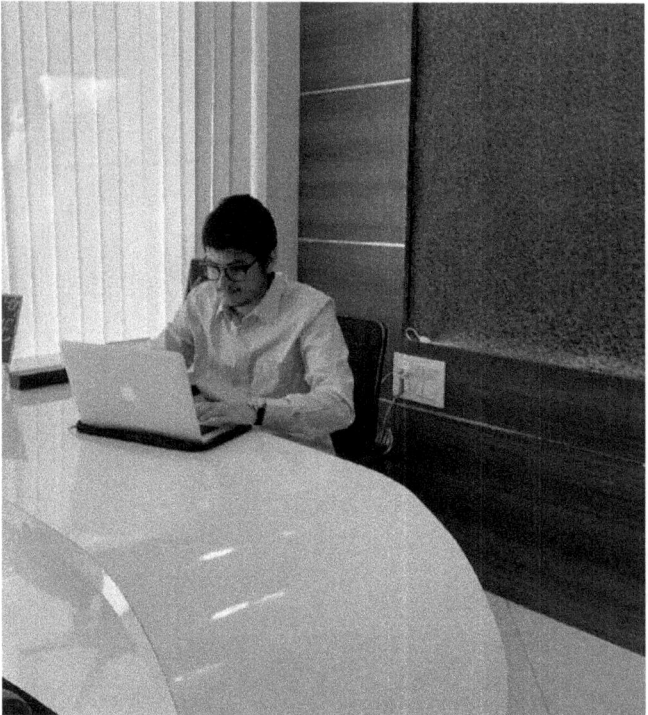

ANSHUL KARWA is the author behind the book STOCK INVESTING. He is a Chartered Accountant, lawyer and done his bachelor in computer applications. His study across multiple courses broadly addresses narratives of human experience. He is from Non-Commerce background and graduated from Christ University. Eventually, he developed an interest in finance and stocks in college. This led him to do one of the most challenging and toughest exams in India – Chartered Accountant. He cleared it in First Attempt being one out of five ninety-two students.


Regards

--

# CA. Anshul Karwa

www.ingramcontent.com/pod-product-compliance
Lightning Source LLC
Chambersburg PA
CBHW071213210326
41597CB00016B/1793